UNDERSTANDING

VLADIMIR NABOKOV

Understanding Contemporary American Literature

Matthew J. Bruccoli, *Editor*

UNDERSTANDING
Vladimir
Nabokov

by STEPHEN JAN PARKER

UNIVERSITY OF SOUTH CAROLINA PRESS

Published in Columbia, South Carolina, by the
University of South Carolina Press

Manufactured in the United States of America

Library of Congress Cataloging-in-Publication Data

Parker, Stephen Jan.
  Understanding Vladimir Nabokov.

  (Understanding contemporary American literature)
  Bibliography: p.
  Includes index.
  1. Nabokov, Vladimir Vladimirovich, 1899–1977—
Criticism and interpretation.   I. Title.   II. Series.
PS3527.A15Z87   1987   813′.54   87-10777
ISBN 0-87249-494-2
ISBN 0-87249-495-0 (pbk.)   NABOKOV

For
Marie-Luce

CONTENTS

EDITOR'S PREFACE

Understanding Contemporary American Literature has been planned as a series of guides or companions for students as well as good nonacademic readers. The editor and publisher perceive a need for these volumes because much of the influential contemporary literature makes special demands. Uninitiated readers encounter difficulty in approaching works that depart from the traditional forms and techniques of prose and poetry. Literature relies on conventions, but the conventions keep evolving; new writers form their own conventions—which in time may become familiar. Put simply, *UCAL* provides instruction in how to read certain contemporary writers—identifying and explicating their material, themes, use of language, point of view, structures, symbolism, and responses to experience.

The word *understanding* in the series title was deliberately chosen. Many willing readers lack an adequate understanding of how contemporary literature works; that is, what the author is attempting to express and the means by which it is conveyed. Although the criticism and analysis in the series have been aimed at a level of general accessibility, these introductory volumes are meant to be applied in conjunction with the works they cover. Thus they do not provide a substitute for the works and authors they introduce, but rather prepare the reader for more profitable literary experiences.

M. J. B.

ACKNOWLEDGMENTS

I would like to thank Véra Nabokov and Dmitri Nabokov for their assistance and trust; Fan Parker for her encouragement; and Marie-Luce, Sandra and Richard for their support and for enduring, with grace and understanding, my endless hours at the Kaypro.

For permission to quote excerpts from the works of Vladimir Nabokov grateful acknowledgment is made to Véra Nabokov.

UNDERSTANDING
VLADIMIR NABOKOV

CHAPTER ONE

Understanding Vladimir Nabokov

Career

Alas! In vain historians pry and probe:
The same wind blows, and in the same live robe
Truth bends her head to fingers curved cupwise; . . .

Fyodor Godunov-Cherdyntsev, *The Gift*

The search for the truth of a life is a preoccupation of Vladimir Nabokov's fiction. The reader learns not to look for it in the ordered linear procession of dates, places, and events which punctuate the passage from birth to death, but to seek it in the intricately patterned design which gives each of us our uniqueness. Nabokov provides an edifying example of how one illuminates such designs in his autobiography, *Speak, Memory*, a work which is highly commended to the reader. For the purposes of this book the skeleton of our writer's life and career will serve adequately.

UNDERSTANDING VLADIMIR NABOKOV

Vladimir Vladimirovich Nabokov was born on April 23, 1899, in the Nabokov town house on 47 Morskaya St., St. Petersburg (now Leningrad), Russia, the first of five children. His father, Vladimir Dmitrievich Nabokov, was a professor of criminal law and a prominent leader of the Constitutional-Democratic Party in prerevolutionary Russia. His mother, Elena Ivanovna Rukavishnikov, was the daughter of a landowner and philanthropist. Their son's early education was entrusted to a series of nurses and tutors in their town house and country estates. Nabokov grew up trilingual—learning first English, then Russian and French—and was a voracious reader with access to the approximately 10,000 titles in his father's library. From 1911–1917 he attended the Tenishev Academy, one of the two most prominent lycées of the Russian capital city. His first literary work, a collection of poems, was privately printed in 500 copies in 1916.

In the aftermath of the Soviet revolution, the Nabokov family went into exile. In 1919 Nabokov enrolled in Trinity College, Cambridge University where he took a degree in Russian and French literatures. Playing goalkeeper on the Trinity College soccer team, rather than long hours never spent in the library, remained Nabokov's fondest memory of this period. Following graduation in

CAREER

1922 he settled in Berlin as a resident alien with the intention of becoming a Russian writer. There in 1925 he met and married Véra Evseevna Slonim, and their only child, Dmitri, was born in 1934. The Nabokovs moved to France in 1937 and then emigrated to America, arriving in New York City in May 1940.

The first European segment of Nabokov's career was highly prolific. Publishing in the leading Russian émigré newspapers and journals of Western and Eastern Europe, he wrote nine novels, forty-eight short stories, several hundred poems, nine plays, many essays, reviews, translations, chess problems, and invented the Russian crossword puzzle. These many publications, however, brought meager financial rewards, which had to be supplemented by private language and tennis lessons.

Arriving in the USA with only $100, Nabokov eventually obtained a modestly remunerated teaching position at Wellesley College (1941–1948) as Visiting Professor of Russian and augmented that with an appointment as Fellow of the Museum of Comparative Zoology, Harvard University, where he happily engaged in lepidopterological studies (1942–1948). In 1945 he became an American citizen, and from 1948–1958 served as a professor at Cornell University, teaching courses on

UNDERSTANDING VLADIMIR NABOKOV

Russian literature as well as his now famous course on the European novel.

Nabokov's mastery of the English language was a remarkable accomplishment which allowed his writing to continue unabated. *The Real Life of Sebastian Knight* (1941), *Bend Sinister* (1947), and the stories and poems which ran regularly in *Atlantic Monthly* and *The New Yorker* launched his career as an American writer. In 1958 the international hubbub surrounding *Lolita* brought him and his writings the world-wide attention they properly deserved. He resigned from Cornell in the fall of 1958 and eventually settled in Montreux, Switzerland, where he resided and continued to write prolifically until his death on July 2, 1977, of cardiac arrest brought on by a viral infection.

Aspects of Nabokov's Fiction

"How small the cosmos (a kangaroo's pouch would hold it), how paltry and puny in comparison to human consciousness, to a single individual recollection, and its expression in words!"

Vladimir Nabokov, *Speak, Memory*

An overview of the characteristics of Nabokov's prose fiction might properly begin with a statement of the fundamental principle upon which his writings and life were based. Two years

ASPECTS OF NABOKOV'S FICTION

after his arrival in America, Nabokov wrote in *The Wellesley Magazine*:

The splendid paradox of democracy is that while stress is laid on the rule of all and equality of common rights, it is the individual that derives from it his special and uncommon benefit. Ethically, the members of a democracy are equals; spiritually, each has the right to be as different from his neighbors as he pleases. . . . Democracy is humanity at its best . . . because it is the natural condition of every man since the human mind became conscious not only of the world but of itself.[1]

Nabokov was a supreme individualist, and the hero of his fictions is always the individual human consciousness left free to either grow in health or expire in misconceived obsession. His art focuses on differences rather than similarities, much the way his scientific interests centered on the taxonomic differentiation of species. Along with the freedom granted his creations, there is also a concommitant accountability. A strong moral vision underlies his art, and Nabokov's reader will discover in his fictions a gentleness and a defense of the weak and the blameless which is joined with "a total honesty on every plane and an utter freedom from anything cruel, cheap, or mean."[2]

In the classroom Nabokov would regularly teach *Bleak House* and *Mansfield Park* while making it clear that he did not necessarily care for other novels by Dickens and Austen. His interest was in the individual work of art rather than the general commonalities of genre or the general evaluations of a writer's entire production. In reference to his own writings he noted that "One of the functions of all my novels is to prove that the novel in general does not exist."[3] By following his own dicta—"a ready-made world unavoidably leads to the ready-made words" and "great writers invent their own worlds"—Nabokov sought to create original, autonomous and finely wrought imagined worlds in each of his novels. Knowledge of one Nabokov work is not a necessary prerequisite for the understanding of another. Like each of his protagonists, each Nabokov novel is invested with a discrete individuality, while as a group they defy simple reduction to a repetitive formula of themes and forms. One can, however, localize several characteristic aspects of his art.

Characters

When Nabokov's first novels appeared in the 1920s and 1930s, many émigré critics termed them alien to the traditions of the great Russian novel because they seemed to lack any commitment to issues which engage the social man. Today it is well understood that the protagonists of Nabo-

ASPECTS OF NABOKOV'S FICTION

kov's fictions are indeed not social beings in the traditional sense. They are from all walks of life—a chocolate merchant, a chess prodigy, a businessman, a professor of Russian, a doll maker, a writer—but it is apparent that none of them is particularly interested in careers, possessions, the acquisition of rank or power. Nor are they concerned with politics, religion, social causes, or current events. Moreover, they appear largely free of the determining forces of environment and heredity and, as such, their behavior cannot be understood by theories of religion, psychoanalysis, or Marxism.[4]

The Russian poet and critic, Vladislav Khodasevich, proposed in 1937 that all of Nabokov's heroes were actually artists in disguise.[5] It would be more correct to say that each of his protagonists is a discreet consciousness liberated from the everyday affairs of social man. Thus freed from the habitual concerns of daily life, the naked consciousness is left free to react to those things upon which consciousness feeds: stimuli of the senses, language, beauty, patterns, disguises, tricks, games, puzzles of various sorts. The central concern of Nabokov's fiction is with the many ways in which an individual's active consciousness shapes reality.

What distinguishes one of Nabokov's characters from another is the degree of intelligence, sensibility, imagination, and creative powers which each one possesses. At one end of the spectrum is the solipsist, mistakenly convinced that reality is entirely his own creation, while at the other end is the free consciousness, delighting in the mystery and wonders of conscious life while striving to "peer beyond its own limits." As for himself, Nabokov wrote that his urge had always been "to fight the utter degradation, ridicule, and horror of having developed an infinity of sensation and thought within a finite existence."[6] The best of his characters fight the same battle and the fascination for author and reader rests with the realities that are discovered.

A separate category of characters is occupied by the "poshlyaki," the embodiments of the varied array of "poshlust" found in his novels. "Ever since Russia began to think . . . educated, sensitive and free-minded Russians were acutely aware of the furtive and clammy touch of 'poshlust',"Nabokov states in his book on Nikolai Gogol.[7] " 'Poshlust'," he goes on to explain, "is not only the obviously trashy but also the falsely important, the falsely beautiful, the falsely clever, the falsely attractive." It is present in advertisements which suggest that "the acme of happiness is purchasable and that its purchase somehow ennobles the pur-

ASPECTS OF NABOKOV'S FICTION

chaser". And it is "especially vigorous and vicious when the sham is *not* obvious and when the values it mimics are considered, rightly or wrongly, to belong to the very highest level of art, thought or emotion." Thus "poshlust" is found in "corny trash, vulgar clichés, Philistinism in all its phases, imitations of imitations, bogus profundities, crude, moronic and dishonest pseudo-literature."[8]

In each instance the philistine poshlyak demonstrates the heavy cost of forfeiting a sentient life. The range is from the inoffensive, humorous and sometimes exhilarating sort, as found for instance in the persons inhabiting the American roadside scenes of *Lolita*, to the banal types who people the world of *The Defense*, to the cruel and destructive types embodied in the characters and worlds of *Invitation to a Beheading* and *Bend Sinister*.

Subjects

Nabokov's primary subject is an ongoing exploration of the forms, functions, powers, and limitations of consciousness. "Being aware of being aware of being," Nabokov wrote, is what distinguishes us from animals. ". . . if I not only know that I *am* but also know that I know it, then I belong to the human species. All the rest follows—the glory of thought, poetry, a vision of the universe."[9] If exiles are prevalent in his fictive world, it is not simply because Nabokov was himself an exile, but because this acute state of displacement and dislocation offers ideal circumstances for consideration of the individual forced to confront past, present, and future, self and setting. If love and sexuality in their many forms are present, it is not because of simple notions of Freudian ideology, but because as universal experiences love and sexuality in their various forms provide enormous stimuli to the individual states and workings of conscious life. In a similar manner, Nabokov repeatedly explores such things as madness, art and the artist to detail the varied workings of individual consciousness.

In a brilliant overview of Nabokov's metaphysics, Brian Boyd observes that its structure has a helical design: "its initial coil is the world of space, the second the world of time, the third the world of human, time-bound consciousness, and the next, if there is another stage, a consciousness beyond time."[10] Nabokov's explorations into the worlds of space, time, consciousness, and possibly consciousness beyond time are abetted by the conjunction of the lessons of science with the methods of art. The gifted author, Nabokov explains, must have the capacity to combine "the passion of the scientist and the precision of the artist." In his fictions the "scientific" facts are

ASPECTS OF NABOKOV'S FICTION

the carefully patterned details which provide the keys as well as the themes to his novels.

It is in lepidopterological work that Nabokov found pleasures even greater than those found in the practice of literature. "My passion for lepidopterological research, . . . is even more pleasurable than the study and practice of literature, . . . The tactile delights of precise delineation, the silent paradise of the camera lucida, and the precision of poetry in taxonomic description represent the artistic side of the thrill which accumulation of new knowledge . . . gives its first begetter."[11] The butterfly is his acknowledged signature, both figuratively and literally (he frequently signed his books with hand-drawn butterflies), and is omnipresent as object and metaphor throughout his writings. Butterflies are explored and thematized in regard to every aspect of their physical being (symmetry, beauty, fragility, mimetic disguise) and activities (migration, metamorphosis).

The study of natural science, Nabokov believed, teaches one how to observe, and careful observation led Nabokov to the conclusion that reality is a wholly subjective matter and that the patterns of the observed world suggest a dimension beyond any conceivable utilitarian purpose. His art proposes to explore the boundaries of reality through the power of imagination. "There is, it would seem, in the dimensional scale of the world a kind of delicate meeting place between imagination and knowledge."[12] He also wrote, "I tend more and more to regard the objective existence of *all* events as a form of impure imagination—hence my inverted commas around 'reality.' Whatever the mind grasps, it does so with the assistance of creative fancy, that drop of water on a glass slide which gives distinctness and relief to the observed organism."[13]

It has been said by some that Nabokov's novels reveal him to be a writer anxious to escape into aesthetics (to borrow the title of Page Stegner's book). It is also said that he is a writer who creates self-enclosed, marvelously detailed worlds which are meant to stand in the place of the real world. Nothing could be further from the truth. Though Nabokov is not the author of "realistic" fiction he is surely the most committed of realists. "You can get nearer and nearer, so to speak, to reality," he wrote, "but you never get near enough because reality is an infinite succession of steps, levels of perception, false bottoms, and hence unquenchable, unattainable."[14] Reality actually remains for Nabokov the inexhaustible source of his fictions.

In order to measure personal reality and one's position in the world of space and time, a person must have recourse to memory. Because one's

ASPECTS OF NABOKOV'S FICTION

Present is constantly becoming one's Past, each of Nabokov's personages takes form through the individual workings of the individual's memories. Ideally, the "supreme achievement" of memory is "the masterly use it makes of innate harmonies when gathering to its fold the suspended and wandering tonalities of the past."[15] This act of retention and recall is, according to Nabokov, "the act of art, artistic selection, artistic blending, artistic recombination of actual events."[16] The protagonists of his fiction seldom fully apprehend these harmonies because of the restrictions and limitations of their visions. But they are there, presented and prefigured by the author, and the act of reading Nabokov's fictions entails their identification and recognition by the reader.

The construction of such "tonalities of the past" also presupposes a certain view of time. "I confess I do not believe in time," Nabokov wrote. "I like to fold my magic carpet, after use, in such a way as to superimpose one part of the pattern upon another."[17] Again, most of Nabokov's characters are unable to do this because they have imprisoned themselves in time. Only a few will share their author's suspicion that the elaborate patterning of man's existence suggests the possibility of a dimension beyond the mortal sense of space, time and consciousness. That Nabokov believed in such a dimension was stated with rare exuberance: "It is . . . when one is wide awake, at moments of robust joy and achievement, on the highest terrace of consciousness, that mortality has a chance to peer beyond its own limits. . . . And although nothing much can be seen through the mist, there is somehow the blissful feeling that one is looking in the right direction."[18] It can be fairly said that all of his art maintains this high perspective.

Techniques

"In a first-rate work of fiction," Nabokov wrote, "the real clash is not between the characters but between the author and the world."[19] Reading Nabokov is a demanding task. One cannot simply go through one of his novels, close its covers, and then proceed to discuss its general ideas. Indeed, as with all fiction of "modernism," a Nabokov novel cannot be read, but must be reread, or better still, re-re-read.

Each of the fictions can be peeled back to reveal successive layers of meaning. Nabokov held that reality was "a very subjective affair" ("I can only define it as a kind of gradual accumulation of information; and as specialization") determined by the figuring power of a given perception.[20] In his novels there are at least three (and frequently

ASPECTS OF NABOKOV'S FICTION

more) differing realities—the protagonist's, the narrator's, and the author's. The identification of the various points of view in each novel is crucial for any understanding of the text. When the narrator and protagonist are the same person, as in the frequently employed first-person singular confessional mode, complications normally derive from the untrustworthiness of the narrator. Hermann, the narrator of *Despair*, for instance, proudly declares that he is an inspired liar and not to be trusted. In each novel, then, the narrative points of view challenge the reader to distinguish between different levels of perception.

The effort of doing so is made all the more difficult because of the reflexive nature of Nabokov's texts. Joseph Frank, in his seminal essay on spatial form in modern literature, first noted that a central characteristic of modern fiction is the replacement of normal cause-effect sequence by word-groups which relate to each other internally, independently of the time sequence of the narrative. Frank explains that a reader cannot apprehend the meaning of a word-group in a modern novel "until the entire pattern of internal references can be apprehended as a unity." Because the word-groups have reference solely within the text, they take on meaning only when finally gathered together and then apprehended instantaneously, as it were, in space. This is a way of saying that modernist fiction, by definition, cannot be read, but only reread, since "a knowledge of the whole is essential to an understanding of any part."[21]

This is fully applicable to the experience of Nabokov's texts. Because the body of a Nabokov work consists of intricately arranged motifs, the reader must discover, follow, and retain the component threads of the motifs in order to identify and understand the major lines of the text. Speaking of the ideal reader of Nabokov's fictions, Carl Proffer suggests that such a person should be the possessor of an eidetic memory.[22] The exercise of locating, retaining, and assembling the components is more than a game, although game-playing is one of the levels of enjoyment in reading Nabokov. As stated by Robert Alter, "the key to any sense of reality, certainly for Nabokov and probably for all of us, is the perception of pattern."[23] Nabokov has a fascination with patterns of every sort as found in the natural world and in the lives of men. His artistic conviction is that the uniqueness of all things resides in their unique designs. It thus follows that access to reality is dependent upon the determination of pattern which is gained by careful observation leading to conscious discovery. Nabokov speaks of his search to reveal the unique and intricate watermark of his

ASPECTS OF NABOKOV'S FICTION

own life in the pages of his autobiography, affirming that "the following of such thematic designs through one's life should be the true purpose of autobiography."[24] So it is with his literary creations. As their creator, Nabokov imbues each fictional life and each fictional world with its patterns and asks the reader to discern them.

Other narrative techniques employed by Nabokov function to remind the reader that the world of his novels is a fiction controlled by the author, and not to be confused with any assumed general "reality" existing outside of the text. The distancing of the reader from the involuted texts while pointing up the artifice of fiction serves to remind one, often in a disturbing way, that fiction is make-believe and that the reader is being controlled by an author. These techniques include appearances by the author's persona within the text, extensive use of the metaphor of staging (exits, entrances, stage directions, props, scenery), the appearance of the same characters in several different works, controlled fateful coincidences, the inclusion of works-within-the-work, the various artifices of narration, and a broad range of parodies. Such techniques not only assert the fictionality of the text, but also serve to unmask overworked clichés, literary conventions, and conditioned reader responses. They educate the reader about the nature of all literary fictions and at the same time establish the originality and independence of the Nabokov text. They also serve to challenge any comfortable notion that a general "reality" exists at all.

Another characteristic of the novels is a profusion of parody and allusion. There are parodies of literary conventions (narrative, structural, stylistic) and literary styles (such as romantic, sentimental, impressionistic); parodies of the themes of fiction (the love story, the detective story, the eternal triangle); parodies of the characters of fiction (the lover, the mother, the writer, the critic). Nabokov enjoys upending the norms in order to revivify them. But parody is not to be confused with satire. "Satire," Nabokov notes, "is a lesson, parody is a game."[25]

Because of the great number of allusions in the texts, primarily literary, Carl Proffer suggests that the ideal reader of Nabokov should also be "a literary scholar trained and widely read in several European languages."[26] The importance of identifying and clarifying these allusions has been well recognized and attempts to do so form a large part of the extensive Nabokov critical bibliography. It has been shown that on occasion the identification of a single allusion can be crucial to the understanding of a text. For example, if the reader fails to recognize that the title of Nabokov's story, "That in Aleppo Once . . . ," comes from a line in Shakespeare's *Othello*, he will fail to understand the import of the concluding lines of that story. The serious point of these games of parody and allusion, as with the distancing devices, is that they serve to set the literary creations (stories, characters, situations) within a line of literary antecedents, in order to distinguish them from prior forms by presenting new perspectives and thus establishing their originality.

Language and Style

Vladimir Nabokov was a masterful writer in three languages and it has been suggested that the greater part of his writings might well be considered "a sort of meditation—lyric, ironic, technical, parodistic—on the nature of human language, on the enigmatic coexistence of different, linguistically generated world visions."[27] The reader of his English writings becomes quickly aware of Nabokov's exceptional powers of expression, of the broad lexical range of his texts, the wide varieties of idiomatic usage, and the variety of stylistic devices.

The reader also quickly discovers that a good dictionary is a handy thing to have when reading Nabokov. Good readers of good literature, Nabokov told his students, need good dictionaries. The use of *le mot juste* takes on special relevance in his prose because words are the very facts of his fiction. Neologisms and archaic terms are not meant to obscure but to clarify. Each word and word-grouping functions to particularize and make specific. Nabokov makes this explicit in the following important remark on visual shades:

When the intellect limits itself to the general notion, or primitive notion, of a certain color it deprives the senses of its shades. In different languages different colors were used in a general sense before shades were distinguished. . . . For me the shades, or rather colors, of, say, a fox, a ruby, a carrot, a pink rose, a dark cherry, a flushed cheek, are as different as blue is from green or the royal purple of blood from the English sense of violet blue. I think . . . students, . . . readers should be taught to *see* things, to discriminate between visual shades as the author does, and not to lump them under such arbitrary labels as "red."[28]

Thus in Nabokov's view the individuation of word categories is no less important than the individuation of human consciousness. It is not unusual for readers of Nabokov's prose to have the feeling that his powers of expression are so exact and complete, and what he seeks to express is so precisely termed, that paraphrase is impossible.

"Art exists so that one may recover the sensation of life," wrote Viktor Shklovsky, the noted

ASPECTS OF NABOKOV'S FICTION

Russian Formalist critic. "People living at the seashore grow so accustomed to the murmur of the waves that they never hear it. By the same token, we scarcely ever hear the words which we utter. . . . We look at each other, but we do not see each other anymore. Our perception of the world has withered away, what has remained is mere recognition."[29] The true purpose of art, Shklovsky reasoned, is to impart the sensation of things as they are perceived, and not as they are known. It is perhaps appropriate to think of Vladimir Nabokov's prose as devoted to this end. Few writers so thoroughly engage the reader's attention upon the specific constituents of reality, the foci of consciousness, as does Nabokov. His art marshals a whole panoply of stylistic usages for the purpose of awakening fresh perception.

Though readers of modern literature have grown accustomed to searching for symbols in the texts of contemporary writers, the urge to do so should be shunned when reading Nabokov. "There exist novelists and poets, and ecclesiastic writers, who deliberately use color terms, or numbers, in a strictly symbolic sense," he wrote. "The type of writer I am, half-painter, half-naturalist, finds the use of symbols hateful because it substitutes a dead general idea for a live specific impression."[30] The thought is clarified further in the only published remarks Nabokov ever directed at a misguided critic of his imaginative writings:

. . . it often happens that a whole paragraph or sinu-ous sentence exists as a discrete organism, with its own imagery, its own invocations, its own bloom, and then it is especially precious, and also vulnerable, so that if an outsider, immune to poetry and common sense, injects spurious symbols into it, or actually tampers with its wording, its magic is replaced by maggots. The various words . . . are not labels, not pointers . . . but live fragments of specific description, rudiments of metaphor, and echoes of creative emo-tion.[31]

It is precisely the abundance of live detail that typifies Nabokov's vision. Consider this one exam-ple, the view of a park as seen from the entry gate:

Trimmed with ferns outside, luxuriantly lined with jasmine and honeysuckle inside, in places darkened by fir needles, in others lightened by birch leaves, this huge, dense and multipathed park stood poised in an equilibrium of sun and shadow, which formed from night to night a variable, but in its variability a uniquely characteristic harmony. If circles of warm light palpitated underfoot in the avenue, then a thick velvet stripe was sure to stretch across in the distance, behind it again came that tawny sieve, while further, at the bottom, there deepened a rich blackness that, transferred to paper, would satisfy the water colorist only as long as the paint remained wet, so that he

ASPECTS OF NABOKOV'S FICTION

would have to put on layer after layer to retain its beauty—which would immediately fade. All paths led to the house, but geometry notwithstanding, it seemed the quickest way was not by the straight avenue, slim and meek with a sensitive shadow (rising like a blind woman to meet you and touch your face) and with a burst of emerald sunlight at the very end, but by any of its tortuous and unweeded neighbors.[32]

The passage is intensely visual, sharply precise and emotionally evocative. The scene is tangible, substantive, complete, and such prose, so carefully and fully fashioned, and so characteristic of Nabokov's writing, needs no purpose other than its own being.

Notes

1. Vladimir Nabokov, "What Faith Means to a Resisting People," *The Wellesley Magazine* (April 1942); cited in Ellen Pifer, *Nabokov and the Novel* (Cambridge, MA: Harvard University Press, 1980) 51.

2. Peter Quennell, *Vladimir Nabokov. A Tribute* (New York: William Morrow, 1980) 128.

3. Vladimir Nabokov, *Strong Opinions* (New York: McGraw-Hill, 1973) 115.

4. These characteristics of Nabokov's heroes were first enumerated and summarized in Jack Handley, "To Die in English," (*Northwest Review*. Spring 1963, 23–40).

5. Vladislav Khodasevich, "On Sirin," Alfred Appel, Jr. and Charles Newman, eds. *Nabokov: Criticism, Reminiscences, Translations, and Tributes* (Evanston, IL: Northwestern University Press, 1970) 96–101.

6. Vladimir Nabokov, *Speak, Memory: An Autobiography Revisited* (New York: G. P. Putnam's Sons, 1967) 297.

7. Vladimir Nabokov, *Nikolai Gogol* (New York: New Directions, 1944) 64–70.

8. *Nikolai Gogol* 68.

9. *Strong Opinions* 142.

10. Brian Boyd, "Nabokov's Philosophical World," *Southern Review* (Adelaide, Australia, November 1981) 260; also, in different form, in Brian Boyd, *Nabokov's ADA: The Place of Consciousness* (Ann Arbor, MI: Ardis, 1985).

11. *Strong Opinions* 78–79.

12. *Speak, Memory* 166–67.

13. *Strong Opinions* 154.

14. *Strong Opinions* 11.

15. *Speak, Memory* 170.

16. *Strong Opinions* 186.

17. *Speak, Memory* 139.

18. *Speak, Memory* 50.

19. *Speak, Memory* 290.

20. *Strong Opinions* 10.

21. Joseph Frank, *The Widening Gyre* (Bloomington, IN: Indiana University Press, 1963) 16–19.

22. Carl Proffer, *Keys to LOLITA* (Bloomington, IN: Indiana University Press, 1968) 5.

23. Robert Alter, "*Invitation to a Beheading*: Nabokov and the Art of Politics," Alfred Appel, Jr. and Charles Newman, eds. *Nabokov: Criticism, Reminiscnces, Translations, and Tributes* (Evanston, IL: Northwestern University Press, 1970) 45.

24. *Speak, Memory* 27.

25. *Strong Opinions* 75.

26. Carl Proffer, *Keys to LOLITA* 5.

27. George Steiner, "Extraterritorial," Alfred Appel, Jr. and Charles Newman, eds. *Nabokov: Criticism, Reminiscences, Translations, and Tributes* (Evanston, IL: Northwestern University Press, 1970) 123–24.

UNDERSTANDING VLADIMIR NABOKOV

28. Alfred Appel, Jr., ed. *The Annotated LOLITA* (New York: McGraw-Hill, 1970) 362.

29. Viktor Shklovsky, "Art as Technique," Lee T. Lemon and Marion J. Reis eds. *Russian Formalist Criticism: Four Essays* (Lincoln, NE: University of Nebraska Press, 1965) 12–13.

30. *The Annotated LOLITA* 362.

31. *Strong Opinions* 305.

32. Vladimir Nabokov, *The Gift* (New York: G. P. Putnam's Sons, 1963) 91.

CHAPTER TWO

Russian Novels

When Vladimir Nabokov left for America in 1940 he abandoned his native tongue. Thereafter he would no longer write in Russian except for an occasional poem. His first nine novels, 1926–1938, written under the penname "V. Sirin," comprise a distinct segment of his collected works. In subsequent years each of these novels was translated into English either by him or else under his close supervision with varying degrees of emendation. *The Defense* (1930/1964) and *Invitation to a Beheading (1938/1959),* for instance, were deemed worthy of literal translation, whereas other novels, such as *Despair* (1936/1966), were extensively altered in their English versions. This twinning of the novels provides a special dimension to Nabokov's art. The English versions are not simply translations in the usual sense of renderings accomplished by a more or less talented second party. They are, rather, authentic, serial incarnations of the originals with artistic integrity of their own.

With only one exception, the Russian novels have a European setting, most frequently the city of Berlin. The characters are for the most part Russian émigrés. Aside from these general similarities, and of course a shared language of expression, the Russian novels are notable for their diversity of themes, characters, and narrative methods.

The novels which have been selected for consideration are: (1) his first novel (*Mary*) which, though imperfect, immediately establishes Nabokov's thematic and stylistic priorities; (2) his third novel (*The Defense*), a remarkable tour de force; and (3) his last three Russian novels (*Despair, Invitation to a Beheading, The Gift*), designated by him for inclusion in the first omnibus edition of his writings, and generally viewed by critics as the best of his Russian works.

Mary

A writer's first novel is often of small interest in comparison with his later, more mature productions. Yet *Mary* is worthy of consideration because it establishes certain characteristics of many of the subsequent fictions. It is immediately evident, for example, that one of the most striking aspects of the novel (written 1925, published 1926) is its compactness and clear structural lines. Unlike the verbal profusion common to many neophyte novelists who overflow with things to say in their first work, *Mary* is a short novel divided into seventeen brief chapters. The time spanned is one week, the cast of characters is small, and the action, in the novel's present time, is restricted for the most part to the rooms, halls, and elevator of a Berlin boardinghouse. Juxtaposed against the limited spatial and temporal dimensions of the present tense are the expansive, unrestricted dimensions of the protagonist's recollections of his youth in Russia. The contrast between the static, spectral existence in present time and the dynamic, enlivened past as recaptured through memory provides the novel's structural frame.

The story line itself is easily related. In the 1920s, in a Berlin boardinghouse inhabited by seven Russian émigrés, a singular fateful coincidence has placed a woman's former lover and present husband in adjoining rooms. The anticipated arrival of the woman triggers a chain of intense recollections in the lover, which range from memories of their first meeting when he was a vacationing sixteen-year-old student to their last correspondence as he was fleeing Russia during the Civil War. Journeys into the past through memory are interspersed with glimpses into the present lives of the émigrés and the daily routine of the boarding house. Ganin, the lover, ultimately resolves to reclaim his Mary, but then abruptly changes his mind as he is setting out to meet her. With newly found energy and "pleasurable excitement" he abandons Berlin and Mary and sets off for the south of France.

A Chekhovian atmosphere of human isolation pervades the depiction of Berlin émigré life. The details which figure importantly are the items of impersonal furniture and meagre personal effects, barren rooms, and characterless surroundings, the soot and hoot of the regularly passing trains, and the pages ripped from a calendar that serve to designate room numbers. Each of the boarding-house characters functions as an isolated unit with seldom any lines of contact. Each is caught in a private dilemma, and only Ganin is able to find a way out.

In his introduction to the English translation, Nabokov speaks of "the sentimental stab of my attachment to my first book" and of the nostalgia which "remain[s] throughout one's life an insane companion."[1] The reference is to memories of Russia and first love which Ganin shares, in certain respects, with the author. Traveling through "the bright labyrinth of memory" (33), Ganin's thoughts roam in rich sensuous detail from the Russian summer countryside to St. Petersburg winters to the Crimea during the Revolution. In rediscovering Mary, Ganin feels he is rediscovering "all his youth, his Russia" (102).

Ganin's decision not to reclaim Mary provides an unexpected ending (frequent in Nabokov's novels) which has been generally understood by commentators as his recognition that "you can't go home again." But a careful reading of the text reveals that the author has something else in mind. Though Ganin's memories are triggered by a snapshot of Mary, and though she is ostensibly their main subject, the actual content of his memories really has little to do with her. Most of the recreated scenes show Ganin alone—before he meets her, when he is going to see her, when he thinks about her, when he is separated from her. Through judicious use of details Nabokov develops the similarities between Ganin's recollected Mary and Ganin's Berlin mistress, Lyudmila, from whom he longs to free himself. Both women are revealed as banal, both carry the odor of a cheap perfume, both are sexually wanton. It is no coincidence that as Ganin leaves for the train station determined to meet his Mary once again "he suddenly remembered how he had gone to say goodbye to Lyudmila, how he had walked out of her room" (113).

What Ganin has really rediscovered is how wondrous it felt to be young and in love. He recognizes that the starlit evening when he sat on a window ledge waiting for the trilling of a nightingale and thinking that he would probably never get to know this girl was "the highest and most important point in his whole life" (47). At that moment he had been supremely alive, fully conscious and wide-open to the world. His recollections have led him to the realization that the attainment of an object is secondary to the desire and anticipation. It is thus fitting that Mary, who gives her name for the title of the book, never appears in it. And rather than representing an abandonment of his past, his decision to move into the future with renewed energy implies that he recognizes that his past remains an ineradicable part of his present if he once again moves into the future with equally wide-open consciousness.

Reading *Mary*, one of Nabokov's most simply structured novels, the perceptive reader should discover that an understanding of his fictions will come only from close attention to carefully constructed motifs—here including travel (train, tram, bicycle), light and shadow, previsions, the cinema.

RUSSIAN NOVELS

Nabokov's first novel demonstrates that its author gives primacy to structure and form, to narrative technique and narrative control. Moreover, *Mary* introduces several of the themes which will recur often in his fiction—the forces of mundane, communal existence, the distressing state of exile, the power of memory and the play of imagination which feeds upon it, the strength of first love, and the exhilaration of a fully conscious life.

The Defense

Written in 1929 and published in 1930, *The Defense* was the first of Nabokov's novels to present a solipsized world configured around a central metaphor. It was in many ways a new departure for the young novelist, but the American reader of the first English version, thirty-four years later, discovered a world which was by then recognizably Nabokovian. The interest in chess and individual obsession and the construction of intricately patterned fictional worlds was in post-*Lolita* days well established.

In the introduction to the English edition, Nabokov refers to the "chess effects" which are planted in the novel. "Their concatenation," he writes, "can be found in the basic structure."[2] His

THE DEFENSE

own interest, not in the playing of chess but in the
composition of chess problems and the "quasi-
musical, quasi-poetical, or to be quite exact,
poetico-mathematical" inspiration that attends the
composition of such problems, are detailed in his
autobiography in the following words which
equate the joys and challenges of chess problem
composition with those of literary composition.

Themes in chess . . . are such devices as forelaying,
withdrawing, pinning, unpinning and so forth; but it
is only when they are combined in a certain way that
a problem is satisfying. Deceit, to the point of diabo-
lism, and originality, verging upon the grotesque,
were my notions of strategy; and although in matters
of construction I tried to conform, whenever possible,
to classical rules, such as economy of force, unity,
weeding out of loose ends, I was always ready to sac-
rifice purity of form to the exigencies of fantastic
content.[3]

In chess problems the competition is not between
the white and black chess pieces, but between the
solitary composer and the hypothetical problem-
solver, "just as in a first-rate work of fiction,"
Nabokov adds, "the real clash is not between the
characters but between the author and the
world."[4]

The hero's obsession with the game of chess
and the author's narrative strategy, which follows

the lines of chess problem composition, give the novel its form. While Luzhin moves to insanity, wherein chess supplants reality, the author plots his hero's demise (in chess problems the black king must always lose) and the reader assumes the place of the hypothetical problem solver whose role is to correctly identify the moves that bring about the inevitable checkmate.

The reader will note that *The Defense* is structured in three distinct sections. The first encompasses Luzhin's childhood up to the point at which his chess genius is recognized and acknowledged; the second presents the events leading up to his collapse at the crucial championship match; the third details his impossible attempts to reenter life and ends with his suicide. As John Updike has pointed out, the sentence in Chapter 4 (71) which provides a sixteen-year transition in Luzhin's life, from childhood to middle-age, "islands the childhood."[5] The childhood then becomes a reference point for the rest of the novel.

In the first fifty-five pages of the book, the upward slope of Luzhin's life, Nabokov details the genesis and power of the chess obsession and establishes the motifs (lines of play) whose recurrences in part three make the novel's ending inevitable. The young Luzhin is unattractive, inattentive, sullen, morose. He is an outsider, scorned

THE DEFENSE

and abused by his schoolmates and wholly incomprehensible to his parents. His amusements are solitary, progressing from fascination with spatial designs on wallpaper, to Sherlock Holmes story plots, card tricks, general mathematics, geometry, jigsaw puzzles and finally to chess, discovered on that "inevitable day when the whole world suddenly went dark" (39). The advent of chess appears to offer him exit from the darkness of one world and entrance to the brilliance of another. In place of cacaphonous complexity he is offered harmonious simplicity.

Luzhin embraces chess as both a defense and an offense against the threats of reality. For a while he succeeds. His talent is recognized by his parents and acknowledged by the public, and he rises to the rank of Grandmaster. However, the child prodigy must grow into the man, and at the crucial championship match with Turati, to whom he has once before lost, the intricate defense he has prepared proves ineffectual before the unexpected, unpredictable lines of attack. Nabokov's treatment of the event makes it clear that chess reality has by now thoroughly supplanted the real world in the consciousness of Luzhin. He has become a two-dimensional character in a two-dimensional world over which he is about to lose control.

The last section of the novel, which enacts his

attempts to reenter the real world, is played by
Nabokov as a reflection of the patterns of the first
part of the novel. The details of his youth begin to
repeat themselves as once again Luzhin is being
led back to chess. He finally recognizes the trap as
he is working through a chess problem written by
his "chess-father," Valentinov.

Luzhin instantly found the key. In this subtle problem
he saw clearly all the perfidy of its author. . . . a trap,
a trap . . . he would be inveigled into playing chess
and then the next move was clear (248–49).

Mirroring the "day when the whole world went
dark" which ended part one, now it is "as if the
whole world had stopped" (251). Luzhin's only
alternative is to resign, "to drop out of the game,"
by plunging from his bathroom window to "the
dark and pale squares" of the chasm below. In
Nabokov's fictions, a no-exit of madness or death
awaits the protagonist whose solipsized construct
of reality is too narowly conceived.

Nabokov remarks in the introduction to the
English version that his novel diffuses a certain
"warmth" and that Luzhin has been found "lov-
able" by readers. If this is so, it is not only because
Luzhin is portrayed as bumbling and helplessly
vulnerable, but also because he is surrounded by a
gallery of philistines who act as foils to his individ-

THE DEFENSE

uality. His father, Luzhin Sr., is an author of boy's books who would have preferred his son to be a musical prodigy along the lines of the accepted clichés. Forced to accept his son's chess genius, he conceives of a novel while listening to *La Traviata*, in which a child prodigy dressed in a sailor suit defeats elderly bearded men and then dies young, in bed, while playing his last match. Luzhin's life defies both the paternal expectations and the literary clichés.

The female interest in the novel, supplied by the woman whom Luzhin humorously woos and eventually weds, is "she," with no name other than "Mrs. Luzhin." She is fittingly not individualized because she is a type drawn from a long line of nineteenth-century Russian literary heroines known for their philanthropic bent. Said "to adore dogs" and be "always ready to lend money" (106), her preconceived notion of an exotic romance with a mysterious chess genius is quickly dispelled. She is forced to the conclusion that "there were probably greater joys than joys of compassion, but that these were no concern of hers" (190). Like her literary predecessors who were determined to make something of their superfluous men, she gives over her life to constructing Luzhin's renovation. It is through her mediation, as she sets about acquiring for Luzhin a new wardrobe, new

quarters, and new interests, that Nabokov introduces a larger array of poshlyaki (in-laws, a psy-
chiatrist, family friends, visitors from the USSR)
and poshly social activities (dancing, soirées, movies, a job in "a commercial enterprise").

The point to be noted here is not that Luzhin is
being given a choice of two different worlds. His
reality by this stage of his existence is so inextrica-
bly solipsized that "he accept(s) this external life as
something inevitable but completely uninterest-
ing," walking "this way and that among people
thought up by his wife" (228). Like the father's
preconceived notion of a music prodigy and the
wife's ill-defined hopes for an exotic romance, the
world of poshlust serves to highlight Luzhin's
individuality.

Valentinov, Luzhin's chess-impressario and
father-surrogate, is representative of a more insid-
ious type of poshlyak. Like Axel Rex, of *Laughter in
the Dark*, and Ferdinand, in Nabokov's story
"Spring in Fialta," Valentinov is a predator. He
uses the young Luzhin for profit, only to abandon
him when age dulls his novelty, and thus his
market value. It is not accidental that on the day
which culminates in his suicide, Luzhin runs
across his "chess-father" once again after a hiatus
of many years. Valentinov would like Luzhin to act
in a chess tournament scene in a B-grade movie

THE DEFENSE

that he has written for "Veritas" films. It is Valentinov who gives Luzhin the slip of paper carrying the chess problem which reveals "all the perfidy of its author" and condemns him to his fate.

The key was found. The aim of the attack was plain.
By an implacable repetition of moves it was leading
once more to that same passion which would destroy
the dream of life. Devastation, horror, madness (246).

The opening line of the novel reads, "What struck him most was the fact that from Monday on he would be Luzhin." The last page of the novel finally reveals Luzhin's first and patronymic names and gives an elegant circularity to the work. The pages of the fiction are thus circumscribed by the naming of the protagonist. In a sense this is proper since it is naming which gives identity to consciousness. The last lines of the novel read, "The door was burst in. 'Alexander Ivanovich, Aleksandr Ivanovich,' roared several voices. But there was no Alexandr Ivanovich." And this too is proper since Luzhin does not and did not exist except in the pages and words of this imagined world.

The Defense is Nabokov's chess novel, but the theme of chess is present in other works. It contributes, for instance, to the title of his second novel, *King*, *Queen*, *Knave*, and figures prominently in *The Gift* and *The Real Life of Sebastian Knight*. The parallel Nabokov draws between the composition of chess problems and the composition of literary works, as exemplified in this novel, clarifies a central aspect of his art. It establishes the relationship between author, characters, and reader. Valentinov's chess problem, like the man, is cold, cunning and readily solved, whereas Nabokov's novel-problems are lively, life-affirming, and resistant to easy solutions.

Despair

Despair, Nabokov's sixth novel, was written in Berlin in 1932, serialized in 1934, and published in book form in 1936. In 1937 Nabokov made a literal translation of the novel into English for a London publisher, but the edition "sold badly and a few years later a German bomb destroyed the entire stock."[6] Nabokov retranslated it in 1965, and this time chose to revise the text.

On the surface—as it is presented, for example, in the plot synopsis preceeding the fifth and final installment of the novel's serial publication—*Despair* is a straightforward tale of greed and murder:

DESPAIR

For months, our narrator Hermann, a narcissistic chocolate merchant, has planned the murder of his double, the wanderer, Felix. His motives: desperation and greed. Hermann is facing bankruptcy; to escape its maws he will kill Felix, change clothes with him, then hide out. When Felix' body is discovered, the police will think it is Hermann who is dead. Eventually Hermann's 'widow' Lydia will collect his life-insurance money and join him in France, where together they shall live in comfort and idleness.[7]

Hermann murders Felix and goes off to France as planned. After a period of nervous expectation he learns that his crime has been uncovered, and as the novel closes the police are about to take him into custody.

At one level *Despair* is thus a simple novel of detection. But as with Dostoevsky's *Crime and Punishment*, a work frequently parodied in *Despair*, this dimension is only the most obvious and ultimately the least interesting. The novel's other levels derive from its complex narrative form. *Despair* is the best early example of Nabokov's sustained use of first-person narrative by an unreliable narrator (the actual first use occurs in the novella, *The Eye*, 1930). This autobiographical mode of narration introduces particular complexities. While removing the sometimes ambiguous relation between authorial and narrative voice found in third-person narratives, first-person narration poses the more difficult problem of ascertaining the veracity and intent of the narrator. In addition, unless a first-person narrative is written in diary form, wherein events are recorded almost immediately after they occur, there is the added problem of the passage of time, because autobiography gazes backwards. The narrator looks into the past and, depending on memory, imagination, and intent, selectively chooses what will be divulged. The results are already known by him before the writing begins.

In *Despair* everything is made most complex because Hermann admits at the outset that he is a talented actor and an inspired liar. Moreover, he has a purpose which can be adduced only at the end of the novel. Thus Hermann's narrative must be approached with caution and each detail must be scrutinized with care. The title of the work may well come to signify the reader's own response as he confronts this highly involuted text.

Unraveling and then turning back upon itself, the novel can be seen to pose a series of questions: (1) Why is Hermann obsessed by the idea of a double? (2) Why must the double be killed? (3) Why does Hermann write his story? (4) Is he a talented, successful writer? (5) What does Nabokov, Hermann's author, think about all of this?

DESPAIR

Surely part of Hermann's despair is sexual. Early in his story he proclaims that his wife adores him. "To her I was the ideal man," he boasts (35). Yet in the passage which immediately follows he describes the aberration which had occurred for the first time several months before his crucial trip to Prague where he discovered Felix, his "double." The description is the single longest passage added by Nabokov to the revised English version of the novel. The reader should note the progression of events. While in bed caressing Lydia, Hermann's "imp Split" stands in the middle of the room and observes. On successive nights, while Hermann is in bed, the imp moves further from the bed, first sitting in an armchair six paces away, then across the room, then to the threshold of the doorway, and finally to the parlor, from which the imp observes Hermann's sexual performance indirectly in the mirror of the wardrobe door. Then one night, while the imp appears to be enjoying the spectacle of Hermann's prowess, Lydia calls out from the bedroom asking Hermann to bring her a book. Up to this point the reader has been led to believe that Hermann has been with his wife. Lydia's summons reveals the true situation. All the while it is the fantasy double who has been in the conjugal bed; Hermann the husband has not (37–39).

Clues are planted throughout the novel which point to an extramarital affair between Lydia and her cousin, Ardalion. Though Hermann never openly acknowledges his wife's infidelity, the reader does sense that Hermann is aware of it. In a conversation with Felix, for example, Hermann casually remarks, "But women . . . now, really, could you name a single one who did not deceive her husband?" (86). Thus in one respect the double provides Hermann with the projection of a preferred self-image, an abnegation of his true self in the face of his marital/sexual despair. Felix, Hermann tells us, mistrusts women, values friendship with men, and is a free-spirited vagabond. But Felix also serves as the end-point of Hermann's self-love, the certainty that he is his own maker, a god unto himself, who knows his unique self and can find it perfectly reproduced in another person. The murder of Felix will serve not only to further his plans to remake his life with Lydia but, more importantly, he is convinced that it will fix his personal immortality as well.

Learning from a newspaper article that the police are seeking him, Hermann concludes that his sole mistake was the careless neglect of a single detail which revealed Felix' true identity. At this late point in the narrative Nabokov switches the point of view away from Hermann for the first time. A letter from Ardalion—correspondence from another person being one of the devices an author can use to shift point of view while in the confessional mode—reveals that the police never for a moment mistook Felix for Hermann. "It is not enough to kill a man and clothe him adequately," Ardalion writes. "A single additional detail is wanted and that is: resemblance between the two" (215). Thus five pages from the novel's end the reader discovers that Felix was not a true visual double and the entire edifice of Hermann's tale threatens to crumble.

Now it becomes clear why Hermann has written his story. Knowing he has been found out in "life," he will write in the hope of succeeding in art. Proceeding from the premise that "the invention of art contain[s] far more intrinsical truth than life's reality" (132), Hermann longs to convince his reader of the truth of his creation ("the pale organisms of literary heroes feeding under the author's supervision swell gradually with the reader's life-blood" (26)). His success will be measured by the degree to which he succeeds in making his reader his accomplice and collaborator. Waiting word of his success in France, he is also awaiting "the moment of an artist's triumph; of pride, deliverance, bliss; was my picture a sensational success or was it dismal flop?" (193).

Though Hermann flaunts his knowledge of literary devices—playing with the reader's expectations, proposing alternate narrative choices, parodying the work of other writers—his "art," like his obsession, is ultimately flawed, and for similar reasons. Hermann seeks and sees only similarities and semblances. He equates death with art. Gazing at the sleeping Felix, he remarks:

his features were motionless . . . the flawlessly pure image of my corpse. . . . In a state of perfect repose [the] resemblance was strikingly evident, and what is death, if not a face at peace—its artistic perfection? Life only marred my double; thus a breeze dims the bliss of Narcissus (25).

Hermann's flawed vision is restricted to surfaces, and his "art" is the reproduction of a two-dimensional, black and white world. His attempt at self-reproduction is based on the impossible assumption of his own reality totally perceived and thus capable of recreating itself. It is fittingly Ardalion, a portrait painter and Lydia's lover, who explains to Hermann that "every face is unique" and that "the artist perceives, primarily, the *difference* between things" (51).

The relationship between art and reality is therefore a central theme of *Despair*. Nabokov, the

DESPAIR

novel's true author, unmasks Hermann's crime and Hermann's art by allowing the depths of reality to show through the narrative. Acknowledging that "the real author is not I, but my impatient memory" (47), Hermann has not fully understood the implications of what he is saying. It is precisely through a series of repetitive, embedded motifs provided by Hermann's recording memory, but undiscerned by him (lilacs, violets, cigarettes, sticks, birch twigs, white dogs, yellow posts, chocolate, and others), that Nabokov reveals to the careful reader the true inadequacy of Hermann's vision and the underlying "reality."[8]

Hermann's tale degenerates into a diary in the last pages, the final entry dated appropriately April 1. Having denied the reality of his life, and the failure of his crime, and not understanding the failure of his art, it is not surprising that he now attempts to dismiss his fate by invoking a further fiction. Leaning out of his hotel window, Hermann proclaims: "This is a rehearsal. Hold those policemen. A famous film actor will presently come running out of this house" (222). But of course Hermann cannot at the same time be speaking out the window and recording his own words. It must be Nabokov himself, the true author, revealing himself and taking up the pen to close the work.

RUSSIAN NOVELS

Invitation to a Beheading

Invitation to a Beheading (written 1934/published 1938/translated 1959) is Nabokov's most abstract novel and one of his major works. The high degree of self-evident artificiality of this "violin in a void,"[9] as Nabokov terms it, has encouraged a broad divergence of reader interpretations. The novel has been variously understood as a fable, a wild parable, a Nabokovian *1984*, an abstract allegory, a utopian satire, a fantastic story.[10]

"In accordance with the law the death sentence was announced to Cincinnatus C. in a whisper. All rose, exchanging smiles" (9). These curious and chilling lines open the novel *in medias res*. Cincinnatus C. has been condemned to death by decapitation for the crime of "gnostical turpitude." With the exception of one scene, the plot action, such as there is, takes place within the confines of the prison fortress where Cincinnatus, the sole prisoner, awaits his execution and ponders his deliverance. The other characters in the novel are a small grotesque assortment whose forms are sometimes literally interchangeable: Roman, Rodion, Rodrig (lawyer, jailer, prison director), Rodrig's little daughter Emmie, M'sieur Pierre the executioner, Cincinnatus's wife and their two crippled children, her family and current lover, Cincinnatus's mother, the prison librarian, and town luminaries (custodian of the city fountains, district superintendent of schools, lion tamer, judge, telegraph chief, parks administrator, director of supplies).

"Gnostical turpitude," Cincinnatus's crime, is synonymous with "opacity," "impenetrability," and "occlusion." In brief, Cincinnatus has been found guilty of being different in a world in which everyone is transparently alike. No other novel by Nabokov, excepting perhaps *Bend Sinister*, presents such a stark juxtaposition between the lone individual and a society that demands conformity under penalty of death. Nabokov acknowledges in his introduction to his English translation that the book was written "some fifteen years after escaping from the Bolshevist regime, and just before the Nazi regime reached its full volume of welcome" (5). It is not difficult to understand this world which punishes nonconformity by execution as a paradigm of the totalitarian state.[11] But it is equally possible to view the novel as a dream, with Cincinnatus and Pierre as two parts of the same individual confronting the nightmare moments in Everyman's life when unreality breaks through.[12] Or again, one can conclude that the novel's central theme is the plight of the artist struggling mightily to find the words to adequately express individual consciousness in a world of oppressive sameness.[13]

Invitation to a Beheading is devoid of lightness and humor. The poshlust embodied in its pages is unrelievedly sinister; the world described is one of "calamity, horror, madness, error" (91). M'sieur Pierre, the exalted executioner, perfectly incarnates and bespeaks its values. His fondest pleasures are "festive music, favorite knick-knacks, such as a camera or a pipe, friendly talks; the bliss of relieving oneself, which some hold to be on a par with the pleasures of love" (153). In Pierre's mouth and through his actions "romance" becomes perversion, "entertainment" becomes the transmittal of terror, "art" becomes lying and cheating, and "soul" does not exist. Marthe, Cincinnatus's wife, is interested only in having sex with everyone, including Cincinnatus's jailors, and then describing her encounters to her husband, while young Emmie, the prison director's daughter and sometime visitor to Cincinnatus's cell, betrays the innocence, purity, and hope for deliverance which Cincinnatus places in her youthfulness. At age thirty, as he awaits his fate, Cincinnatus is forced to conclude that he has lived all these years "among spectres that appear solid to the touch" (70).

The gradually expanding theme of individual-

INVITATION TO A BEHEADING

ity and the possible existence of another world develops on a line parallel to the unfolding exposition of Pierre's world. Cincinnatus is more and more involved in a search for self-definition, a process which had begun years earlier when he first recognized that he was different from others. Sensing that there must exist another reality which would account for his separateness, he struggles to fix his individuality. "I know something, but expression of it comes so hard. . . . I have no desires, save the desire to express myself—in defiance of all the world's muteness" (91). But he lacks, he says, the proper words to do so. "Those around him understood each other at the first word, since they had no words that would end in an unexpected way" (26). In a world in which everything has a name, "*that which does not have a name does not exist*" (26). Conversely, there are no words to account for mystery, doubt or the expression of individual consciousness.

In his waking life we have "a poor, vague Cincinnatus . . . trusting, feeble and foolish." But in his dreams Cincinnatus removes his outer layers and reaches "the final, indivisible, firm radiant point, and this point says: I am! like a pearly ring embedded in a shark's gory fat" (90). If life is a sham, as it is in the waking world, then it follows that dream is reality. In an often quoted passage

RUSSIAN NOVELS

Cincinnatus dreams of the world which must exist simply because there must be something to account for his being: "There, *tam*, *là-bas*, there the gaze of men glows with inimitable understanding; there the freaks that are tortured here walk unmolested . . . there shines the mirror that now and then sends a chance reflection here" (94).

As Cincinnatus sits in his cell at the beginning of Chapter Eleven, the precise middle of the book, the narrator addresses the reader directly. "The subject will now be the precious quality of Cincinnatus; his fleshy incompleteness." There then follows the longest paragraph of the novel, nearly two pages in length, which describes Cincinnatus's physical being. Though it is not necessary to quote the passage in its entirety, this substantial segment adequately conveys the narrator's dedicated yet futile attempt to capture Cincinnatus.

Cincinnatus's face, grown transparently pallid, with fuzz on its sunken cheeks and a mustache with such delicate hair texture that it seemed to be actually a bit of disheveled sunlight on his upper lip; Cincinnatus's face, small and still young despite all the torments, with gliding eyes . . . of changeable shade . . . completed a picture . . . produced as it was of a thousand barely noticeable, overlapping trifles: of the light outline of his lips, seemingly not quite fully drawn but touched by a master of masters; of the fluttering movements of his empty, not-yet-shaded-in-hands; of

INVITATION TO A BEHEADING

the dispersing and again gathering rays in his animated eyes; but even all of this, analyzed and studied, still could not fully explain Cincinnatus: it was as if one side of his being slid into another dimension, as all the complexity of a tree's foliage passes from shade into radiance, so that you cannot distinguish just where begins the submergence into the shimmer of a different element. . . . everything about him breathed with a delicate, drowsy, but in reality exceptionally strong, ardent and independent life: his veins of the bluest blue pulsated; crystal-clear saliva moistened his lips; the skin quivered on his cheeks and his forehead, which was edged with dissolved light . . . and all this so teased the observer as to make him long to tear apart, cut to shreds, destroy utterly this brazen elusive flesh, and all that it implied and expressed, all that impossible, dazzling freedom'' (120–22).

As pointed out by Robert Alter, the reader is being invited into the writer's laboratory for a demonstration ("the subject will now be . . .").[14] The subject being examined, though invested with a richness of minute and specific detail, remains stubbornly elusive and ultimately unknown. The passage serves as an emphatic statement and example of the absolute discreteness of an individual, and a demonstration of the strengths and limitations of the healthy inquiring artistic imagination which seeks "to know" but which can never know entirely.

In contradistinction, the passage that follows in the text presents the epitome of artistic expression in Pierre's world. The novel *Quercus*, "the best that [Cincinnatus's] age had produced," "the acme of modern thought," (Quercus being the Latin for "oak") is a record of events which had transpired over six hundred years within view of the tree as recorded by "the author sitting with his camera somewhere among the topmost branches" (123). As Alter first pointed out, this is a description of the naturalistic novel taken to absurdity. The controlling assumption is that reality *is* its surface manifestations and that art is but a mechanical record of them. Thus the "photohoroscope" of little Emmie—which projects her entire future life—consists of a series of photographs which record a progressively aging body in preestablished locales and dress. Nothing is unknown.

Believing that he has a unique dimension, Cincinnatus seeks the words which can express it, "not knowing how to write, but sensing with my criminal intuition how words are combined, what one must do for a commonplace word to come alive" (93). He does not succeed, but he has recognized that this is what written art should express. As the text evolves, moving him nearer and nearer to his execution, Cincinnatus moves closer and closer to his liberation. The various

INVITATION TO A BEHEADING

cinematic and stage effects employed throughout the novel (twenty rapidly moving short chapters, stage directions for the entry and exit of various players, carefully staged scenarios with detailed settings and props) provide the entirely appropriate form for this mock world and prepare the reader for the surrealistic execution scene which ends it. Pierre's ax descends and then Cincinnatus rises to watch as the cardboard world collapses. "Everything was coming apart. Everything was falling . . . and amidst the dust, and the falling things, and the flapping scenery, Cincinnatus made his way in that direction where, to judge by the voices, stood beings akin to him" (223).

It is paradoxical that this most artificial of Nabokov's fictions, which so clearly elucidates and exemplifies his artistic credo and practice, should be a favorite of readers who in other contexts consider him a cold and sterile stylist. Whether one understands *Invitation to a Beheading* as a political work, the story of Everyman, or an explanation of the writer's arduous task of naming the unnamed, it is manifestly apparent that its unambiguous hero is individual human consciousness, lovingly conceived and defended, and that one of its "messages" is that while art can describe and probe and suggest, it can never fully account for or replace "reality."

RUSSIAN NOVELS

The Gift

Nabokov considered *The Gift* the best of his Russian novels.[15] It was written in Berlin (1935–37) and then published serially in an expurgated version (1937–38). The complete Russian text was first published in 1952, and the English translation in 1963.[16] The title has several resonances in the novel, but it refers first and most importantly to the gift conferred upon its protagonist. Unlike Hermann, the failed artist of *Despair*, or Cincinnatus, the would-be artist of *Invitation to a Beheading*, Fyodor Godunov-Cherdyntsev, the hero of this novel, is endowed with the rarest gift of creative imagination and literary aptitude. *The Gift* is centrally the story of the development and maturation of a uniquely talented writer. But it is also a compelling love story and an examination and rebuttal of a traditional view of nineteenth-century Russian literature.

The novel consists of five nearly discreet chapters of equal size, with an ending which spirals back to the beginning. On the last pages Fyodor is preparing to write the very novel which the reader has just read. The point of view shifts between first and third person narration, between the recording consciousness learning and discovering, and the omniscient consciousness already aware of out-

THE GIFT

comes and engaged in writing the novel. Moveover, the reader not only reads the novel Fyodor is finally prepared to write, but also several works-within-the-work, including a complete biography of Nikolai Chernyshevsky, a nineteenth-century Russian writer and critic; an incomplete biography of Fyodor's father; some of Fyodor's best poems; separate vignettes on émigré life; and several imagined discourses.

In an essay on Pushkin, Nabokov wrote: "Is it possible to imagine in its full reality the life of another, to relive it in oneself and transfer it intact to paper? I doubt it, for it is only the versimilar and not the true that our spirit and mind perceives."[17] *The Gift* is very much concerned with the possibility of apprehending a life in language, and Fyodor's growth as a writer can be profitably examined from the perspective of his attempts to do so. As the reader moves through the text he will first find Fyodor eliciting his childhood through poetry; then seeking the truth of his father's life; then constructing the imagined life and demise of an acquaintance; writing and publishing a creative biography of Chernyshevsky; and, finally, completing his own autobiography which is Vladimir Nabokov's novel.

The extracts from the fifty poems devoted to Fyodor's childhood, encompassed by the rolling ball that is lost in the first poem and then rediscovered in the last, are embedded in prose. The verses given represent Fyodor's mature work, the product of a long apprenticeship during which his poetry evolves from simple rhymes to complex language and imagery. The prose which surrounds and helps to explain the poetry serves to demonstrate the greater clarity and precision that prose permits. The juxtaposition of poetry and prose demonstrates the nature of both forms, as well as their interrelationship, and suggests why Fyodor evolves from poet to prose writer. Fyodor ultimately strives to create poetic prose in which "thought and music are conjoined." The book of poems serves as his farewell to poetry as a full-time endeavor, though poetic prose will figure significantly elsewhere in the text. In a sense it is also a farewell to his childhood which "has disappeared into a distance even more remote than that of our Russian North,"[18] though the fruits of that childhood, his poems and his gift, have ripened and remain with him.

Nabokov's understanding of the relationship between art and science is nowhere better stated and explained than in Chapter Two, which chronicles Fyodor's attempt to write a biography of his father, an intrepid naturalist who was constantly engaged in fabulous expeditions into uncharted

THE GIFT

regions of Asia, where he was "happy in that incompletely named world in which at every step he named the nameless" (131). Fyodor cherishes lessons taught and examples set by this man whom he rarely saw, and his father holds a powerful sway on the young man and artist. From him Fyodor has learned to appreciate "the incredible artistic wit of mimetic disguise" and to distinguish "the eternally indistinguishable." He was, in brief, taught how to see, how to bring "knowledge-amplified love" to the act of observation, a talent which is indispensable to a writer.

Though Fyodor's father had no use for anthropology and folklore, the reader learns that he did have one favorite Kirghiz fairy tale which has important bearing on Fyodor's (and Nabokov's) art. It is the story of the son of a great khan who falls in love with a young girl he chances to see. As bride-money the young man offers the girl a gold nugget as large as a horse's head. She responds by giving him a thimble-sized bag, asking him to fill it up. He pours all his coins into the bag, and then all the riches of his father's kingdom, but the bag remains unfilled. The girl's mother finally explains that the bag is really a human eye which "wants to encompass everything in the world," and then she takes "a pinch of earth and filled up the bag immediately" (146). The morals are clear: the eye is an all-devouring organ and there is immeasurably more wealth to be obtained (observed) in nature than to be found in worldly riches. The natural world—that is, "reality,"—closely and lovingly observed, endlessly revealing, holds the greatest wealth, and thus the artist, like the scientist, in this most fundamental sense is a realist mining an inexhaustable lode.

Fyodor eventually recognizes that he cannot write a biography of his father because he cannot know the reality of a life which was so much concealed from him. This is implicitly acknowledged when, while narrating his father's last expedition, the narrative voice shifts subtly from "he" to "we" to "I" (134–36). It is Fyodor's tacit admission that all along he has been fictionalizing, that he has been writing *his own* personal and heavily romanticized fantasy, rather than the truth, ultimately unknowable, of his father's very private life.

Fyodor does not write his father's story, nor the story of an acquaintance's suicide. The latter tale is too banal, he decides, though the very process of pursuing the possibility provides the reader an indelible portrait of a well-worn triangular situation. The search for a suitable subject to which he can apply his gift ends with the chance reading of several pages from Nikolai Chernyshevsky's youthful diary. Exposed to its author's "drolly circumstantial style . . . the passion for semicolons, the bogging down of thought in midsentence and the clumsy attempts to extricate it . . . the knight-moves of sense in the trivial commentary" (206), Fyodor is astounded by the impossibility of reconciling the prose and the mental processes it reveals with the reputation and public perception of the historic figure. The incongruence compels Fyodor to learn more about this person who so profoundly affected nineteenth and twentieth-century Russian thought and literature.

Nikolai Gavrilovich Chernyshevsky (1828–1889) was a leading Russian radical-utilitarian critic in mid-nineteenth-century Russia, a contemporary of Dostoevsky, Turgenev and Tolstoy. He was educated at theological school and at the University of St. Petersburg and served on the staff of the journal, *The Contemporary*. He was arrested for radical political activities in 1862, exiled to Siberia in 1863, and returned to his native Saratov only after 1883 to live there until his death in 1889. His aesthetic views were embodied in works of nonfiction, *Studies in the Age of Gogol* (1885–1886) and *The Aesthetic Relations of Art and Reality* (1855), and in one novel, *What Is to Be Done?* (1863).

In Chapter Four these aesthetic views are revealed as the antithesis of Fyodor's. The reader need only compare the lessons of Fyodor's father and the import of the Kirghiz fairy tale with the fundamental tenet of Chernyshevsky's practice of criticism.

We see a tree; another man looks at the same object. We see by the reflection in his eyes that his image of the tree looks exactly the same as our tree. Thus we all see objects as they really exist'' (255).

The reasoning is uncomfortably close to the principle which governs art in the world of *Invitation to a Beheading*. Fyodor nicely remarks, "Like words, things also have their cases. Chernyshevsky saw everything in the nominative" (251).

There is naturally a dimension of *The Gift* that is more readily accessible to a reader versed in the history of Russian letters. Fyodor's several imagined dialogues with Koncheyev, the references to Gogol, Lermontov, and Pushkin in Chapter Four, and allusions to Russian literary affairs at other moments in the text will be of greater interest and import to a knowledgeable audience (such as the Russian émigrés who were the novel's first audience). Nonetheless, *The Gift* is by no means a work accessible only to specialists and the reader does not need special credentials to comprehend the distinctions between Fyodor's views and those of

THE GIFT

Chernyshevsky. Moreover, Chernyshevsky's life, though encased in fiction, becomes paradoxically the finest actual biography of the man yet written and also the best example, in microcosm, of Nabokov's concept of biography.

The sources from which Fyodor quotes are actual, aside from Strannolyubski (Strangelove) who is Fyodor's creation. The form in which the life is drawn is original. Rather than the standard, fleshed-out chronology of dates, places, and events, Fyodor's work derives its living form from the "tamed" *themes* of Chernyshevsky's life—writing exercises, tears, traveling, near-sightedness, pastry shops, officers, spectacles, and so forth. Using the lessons learned from his father Fyodor gleans the details which patterned Chernyshevsky's existence and then unrolls the fabric of the man's life. Ironically, it is through the accumulation and recombination of details that Fyodor succeeds in unmasking this most "myopic materialist" for whom details had always been "merely the aristocratic element in the nation of our general ideas" (259). "Only myopia," Nabokov wrote, "condones the blurry generalizations of ignorance. In high art and pure science detail is everything."[19]

The novel is enormously rich in potential discoveries for the careful reader. There is a wealth of parody, directed, for example, at literary criticism, social mores, émigré life, bad literature, varying degrees of poshlust. On the whole *The Gift* occupies a special place among the full range of the novels. Along with John Shade, the author of the poem, "Pale Fire," Fyodor is the most "normal" of Nabokov's protagonists. Shade is not the narrator of his story and thus is known only from his poem and the testimony of others. But Fyodor presents himself directly. He is not obsessed or deranged, nor does he appropriate the world through the restricted lens of solipsism. On the contrary, because he is a specially gifted artist his perceptions are authentic and prized. No other novel by Nabokov so resembles in tone and content his own autobiography, *Speak, Memory.* The reader will find in Fyodor's beliefs many of the values and opinions of his author, though the reader should be careful not to confuse the fictitious Fyodor with Vladimir Nabokov.

The novel serves as a guidebook which explains and demonstrates the maturation of a healthy, creative, gifted consciousness. The sequence at the end of Chapter Five, in which Fyodor leads the reader into the forest ("Give me your hand, dear reader. . . ." (343)) to create a modern pastoral from a barren landscape, culminates in a rare transcendental moment in which Fyodor imagines that his conscious self has dissolved and merged with the larger reality. It is a passage of rare beauty in which the breaking of mortal bonds is envisioned by Fyodor's consciousness.

I gradually felt that I was becoming moltenly transparent, that I was permeated with flame and existed only insofar as it did. As a book is translated into an exotic idiom, so was I translated into sun. . . . My personal I, the one that wrote books, the one that loved words, colors, mental fireworks, Russia, chocolate and Zina— had somehow disintegrated and dissolved . . . it was now assimilated to the shimmering of the summer forest . . . (345–46).

This exhilarating feeling is a manifestation of Fyodor's love, as is his belief that consciousness knows that another dimension exists beyond the barriers of thought.

. . . the seams and sleaziness of the spring day, the ruffle of the air, the coarse, variously intercrossing threads of confused sounds—was but the reverse side of a magnificent fabric, on the front of which there gradually formed and became alive images invisible to him. (326).

The love shared by Fyodor and Zina is unique in Nabokov's novels. Though one cannot doubt the sincerity of Humbert's love for Lolita and Van's and Ada's love for each other in *Ada*, those are loves which are compromised by their destructive effects on others. The love between Fyodor and Zina epitomizes the ideal union of two separate individuals in which the discreteness of neither is violated ("and not only was Zina cleverly and elegantly made to measure for him by a very painstaking fate, but both of them, forming a single shadow, were made to the measure of something not quite comprehensible, but wonderful and benevolent and continuously surrounding them" (189)). The novel Fyodor plans to write and which the reader has just read, encompassed and enlivened by the story of their love, is Fyodor's gift to Zina, his muse. The prose poems begun in chapter 3 (168–69, 188–89) and completed in the novel's last paragraph link this love, his father, Zina, and his art in a pledge to the future.

Love only what is fanciful and rare; what from the distance of a dream steals through; what knaves condemn to death and fools can't bear. To fiction be as to your country true . . . (168).

. . . and no obstruction for the sage exists where I have put The End: the shadows of my world extend beyond the skyline of the page, blue as tomorrow's morning haze—nor does this terminate the phrase (378).

RUSSIAN NOVELS

Notes

1. Vladimir Nabokov, *Mary* (New York: McGraw-Hill, 1970) xii. Further references will be noted parenthetically.

2. Vladimir Nabokov, *The Defense* (New York: G. P. Putnam's Sons, 1964) 9. Further references will be noted parenthetically.

3. Vladimir Nabokov, *Speak, Memory: An Autobiography Revisited* (New York: G. P. Putnam's Sons, 1967) 288–89. For a selection of chess problems composed by Nabokov, see Vladimir Nabokov, *Poems and Problems* (New York: McGraw-Hill, 1971); for a detailed discussion of the chess theme and chess strategies in Nabokov's works, see D. Barton Johnson, *Worlds in Regression: Some Novels of Vladimir Nabokov* (Ann Arbor, MI: Ardis, 1984).

4. *Speak, Memory* 290.

5. John Updike, "Grandmaster Luzhin," *The New Republic* 151 (26 Sept. 1964): 16.

6. Vladimir Nabokov, *Despair* (New York: G. P. Putnam's Sons, 1965) 8. Further references will be noted parenthetically.

7. Vladimir Nabokov, "*Despair*: Fifth Installment," *Playboy* April 1966; 151.

8. For further discussion of the novel's motifs see, for example, Stephen Suagee, "An Artist's Memory Beats All other Kinds: An Essay on *Despair*," *A Book of Things About Vladimir Nabokov*, ed. Carl Proffer (Ann Arbor, MI: Ardis, 1974) and Claire Rosenfield, "*Despair* and the Lust for Immortality," *Nabokov: The Man and His Work*, ed. L. S. Dembo (Madison, WI: University of Wisconsin Press, 1967). For information regarding allusions in the work see William C. Carroll, "The Cartesian Nightmare of *Despair*," *Nabokov's Fifth Arc*, ed. J. E. Rivers and Charles Nicol (Austin, TX: University of Texas Press, 1982).

9. Vladimir Nabokov, *Invitation to a Beheading* (New York: Capricorn Books, 1959) 7. Further references will be noted parenthetically.

10. See, for example: Burns Singer, "Utopia and Reality," *Encounter* Jan. 1961: 77; John Wain, "Nabokov's Beheading," *The New Republic* 21 Dec. 1959: 19; Ronald Bryden, "I, Cincinnatus," *The Spectator* 3 June 1960: 810; Benjamin De Mott, "Monge or Other Destinations," *Hudson Review* Winter 1960: 620.

RUSSIAN NOVELS

11. Robert Alter, *"Invitation to a Beheading*: Nabokov and the Art of Politics,"* Appel and Newman, eds. *Nabokov: Criticism, Reminiscences, Translations and Tributes* (Evanston, IL: Northwestern University Press, 1970) 41–59.

12. P. M. Bitsilli, "The Revival of Allegory," Appel and Newman, eds. *Nabokov: Criticism, Reminiscences, Translations and Tributes* (Evanston, IL: Northwestern University Press, 1970) 102–18.

13. See, for example, D. Barton Johnson, "The Alpha and Omega of *Invitation to a Beheading*," *Worlds in Regression: Some Novels of Vladimir Nabokov* (Ann Arbor, MI: Ardis, 1985) 28–46.

14. Robert Alter, *"Invitation to a Beheading*: Nabokov and the Art of Politics," 54–55.

15. "It is the longest, I think the best, and the most nostalgic of my Russian novels." Vladimir Nabokov, *Strong Opinions* (New York: McGraw-Hill, 1973) 13.

16. The Russian original of *The Gift* was first serialized in 1937–38 with chapter 4 omitted. The editor of the journal which carried the novel decided that the biography of Chernyshevsky was inappropriate for publication, and thus the complete text did not appear until 1952.

17. Vladimir Nabokov, "Pouchkine ou le vrai et le vraisemblable," *La Nouvelle Revue Française* (March 1937); cited in Andrew Field, *Nabokov: His Life in Art* (Boston: Little, Brown, 1967) 14.

18. Vladimir Nabokov, *The Gift* (New York: G. P. Putnam's Sons, 1963) 38. Further references will be noted parenthetically.

19. Nabokov, *Strong Opinions* 168.

CHAPTER THREE

American Novels

Vladmir Nabokov wrote eight novels in English, 1941–1974. At the time of his death in 1977 he had nearly completed work on a ninth. As with the Russian novels, the English works present autonomous worlds which have individual settings, narrative structures, and thematic concerns. The following commentary considers the four works—*Lolita*, *Pnin*, *Pale Fire*, *Ada or Ardor*—that are the best known and most read, and are generally considered the finest of Nabokov's American novels.

Lolita

Refused by four American publishing houses because of its subject matter, *Lolita* was first published in France in 1955 as a two-volume edition in the English language Traveller's Companion series of Olympia Press. Following protracted and heated

AMERICAN NOVELS

controversy in the British and French media over whether the work was or was not pornographic and should or should not be banned, the first American edition appeared in 1958 and *Lolita* quickly moved to the top of the best-seller lists.[1] While the broad American reading public was belatedly discovering Nabokov, Nabokov was finally gaining the financial rewards which would allow him to resign his teaching position at Cornell in order to write full-time, not only new works but English translations of nearly all his previous Russian fiction.

Appearing frequently on lists of best twentieth-century works, *Lolita* has been termed "the supreme novel of love in the twentieth century"[2] and is generally recognized as the finest of Nabokov's novels and a classic of contemporary literature. It is biography, detective story, tale of the double, romantic novel, travel book, comedy, but also tragedy, and its opening lines—"Lolita, light of my life, fire of my loins. My sin, my soul. Lo-lee-ta: the tip of the tongue taking a trip of three steps down the palate to tap, at three, on the teeth. Lo. Lee. Ta." (11)—herald a work of rare verbal exuberance. *Lolita* was a special favorite of Nabokov's and the only one of his English novels which he himself translated into Russian (1967). As he explained, "I am pursuing a very simple aim: I

LOLITA

want my best English book . . . to be translated correctly into my native language."[3]

The first of Nabokov's novels with an American setting, *Lolita* actually had its first echoes in several Russian stories, *The Gift*, and the 1939 novella, *The Enchanter*.[4] The author himself dated the "first little throb" to Paris in late 1939 or early 1940. "As far as I can recall, the initial shiver of inspiration was somehow prompted by a newspaper story about an ape in the Jardin des Plantes, who, after months of coaxing by a scientist, produced the first drawing ever charcoaled by an animal: this sketch showed the bars of the poor creature's cage."[5] That no one has yet been able to locate such a story in a Paris newspaper is incidental. Nabokov's remark serves properly to point the reader's attention to the bars, actual and metaphorical, which imprison his hero and are the subject of his tale.

Though the novel has two numbered parts, the second beginning after Humbert's and Lolita's first night together, the structural frame of the novel is a series of extended travels. Humbert's life is striking for the absence of repose within it. He moves compulsively through space and time on an impossible quest. Born 1910 in Paris of half-English and half-Dutch parentage, Humbert travels to the seashore in 1923 and meets and falls agonizingly in

AMERICAN NOVELS

love with Annabel Leigh, a girl a few months his junior. Unable to satisfy his urgent sexual desires, the "rift" in his life begins. He marries in 1935, divorces in 1939, suffers several bouts of insanity, joins an expedition to the Arctic, and finally travels to America on the modest financial bequest of a relative. He finds himself at 342 Lawn St., Ramsdale, New England, where at the residence of the widowed Charlotte Haze, on May 30, 1947, he glimpses her twelve-year-old daughter, Dolores (Lolita) Haze, and instantly recognizes in her the ideal embodiment of the "nymphet" which he has been seeking for twenty-five years. He subsequently marries Charlotte; she conveniently dies fifty days later; and Humbert is left the guardian of orphaned Lolita.

On August 15, 1947, he removes Lolita from summer camp and spends his first night with her at "The Enchanted Hunters Inn" where, in an unexpected reversal of roles, she seduces him. Hum and Lo then spend the next year, mid-August 1947 through mid-August 1948, traveling the roads of America. In the fall of 1948 Humbert enrolls Lo in the Beardsley School for Girls, Beardsley, New England. In the spring of 1949, fearing that her participation in a school play ("The Hunted Enchanters") could lead to amorous entanglements with others, Humbert again takes her on

LOLITA

the road. Heading for Hollywood, they only get as far as the western town of Elphinstone where Lolita mysteriously disappears.

Believing that he had been followed and that Lo's disappearance had been carefully contrived, Humbert backtracks the 1,000 miles of their journey seeking clues to the identity of her abductor. This "cryptogrammic paper-chase," as he calls it, from one hotel register to another, turns up many clues, but none give up the secret. Arriving back in Beardsley he hires a private detective, destroys the remaining vestiges of his life with Lolita, has another bout of insanity, reads poetry, and indulges his nympholepsy by haunting playgrounds and beaches. In the summer of 1950 he and Rita, a thirty-year-old vagabond, set out to travel the roads of America, with brief stays in New York and Cantrip College where Humbert is known as a poet and philosopher. In early September 1952 a letter from Lolita sends Humbert on an 800-mile drive to her home where he encounters his Lolita metamorphosed into the seventeen-year-old, married, and pregnant Mrs. Richard F. Schiller. His declaration of love unequivocally rebuffed, the identity of her abductor now confirmed, Humbert drives back to Ramsdale for gun and address, travels to Pavor Manor and murders Clare Quilty. Following his arrest he spends fifty-six days hurriedly writing his story before dying suddenly of a heart attack on November 16, 1952. Thirty-nine days later, on Christmas day, Lolita dies in childbirth.

Nabokov's use of the first person confessional mode of narration once again raises questions not unlike those posed in *Despair*: who is the narrator, why is he writing his tale, how reliable is his narration? Humbert Humbert (a pseudonym that suggests his duality and, in its permutations—H. H., Humbert the Hummer, Humbert the Humble, Humbert the Terrible, and many more—his various guises) is a witty, well-read, middle-aged nympholept who has several reasons for writing his story: (1) to prepare a defense for his murder trial; (2) to explain his special type of passion; (3) to attempt to expiate his sins; (4) to immortalize his beloved Lolita. He is not an inspired liar and the veracity of the reported events seems not to be in doubt. Yet Humbert's interpretations and self-knowledge must be questioned in order to understand the criminal limitations of his narrowly solipsized world. Humbert, after all, is a murderer, and despite the sincerity of his passion and the wittiness of his style Nabokov intends no salvation for him. It should become abundantly clear to the reader that the text is too carefully structured and too polished to be simply the rough journal which, we are told, Humbert began to write frenetically in

LOLITA

a psychiatric ward and then completed in prison fifty-six days later.

The movement of the narrative tracks the progression of Humbert's obsession from general to specific, passive to active, observation to violation. Seeking to rediscover Annabel, his "Riviera love," Humbert's quest covers twenty-five years of voyeurism and madness until his long-standing pederosis culminates in "she, *this* Lolita, *my* Lolita, [who] has individualized the writer's ancient lust, so that above and over everything there is—Lolita" (47). Until he appropriates her from summer camp she remains "safely solipsized." Even after his first Lolita-as-ideal-nymphet induced masturbation (part 1, chapter 13) he is aware that "Lolita was safe and I was safe. What I had madly possessed was not she, but my own creation, another, fanciful Lolita—perhaps more real than Lolita; overlapping, encasing her; floating between me and her, and having no will, no consciousness—indeed, no life of her own" (64).

Writing in the present tense of the narrative, Humbert has understood, too late, that it is only in this form, as the pure product of the imagination, frozen in space and time, that the nymphet actually exists. After providential Fate has provided him the circumstances which allow him to move from observer to violator, the text records his abuses of Lolita (physical, emotional, and moral), all masked in the play of his wit and the humorous tone of the text, and all done in the name of love. Though he never shows contrition for the murder of Quilty, Humbert will eventually, with difficulty and the gift of hindsight, painfully acknowledge that his cross-country jaunts with Lolita were something other than an idyll, punctuated as they were by "her sobs in the night—every night, every night—the moment I feigned sleep" (177–78). Despite his pretty disavowal, "no killers are we. Poets never kill" (90), Humbert is guilty of taking two lives.

He calls Clare Quilty, the man whom he murders, a "semi-animated, subhuman trickster." Quilty is a playwright and a pornographer. Mrs. Vibrissa is his housekeeper, a three-breasted woman is a house guest, and a unique erotic collection is his dearest possession. For his part, Quilty claims that he is "practically impotent," and that Lolita, with whom he says he never had sexual relations, was actually saved by him from "a beastly pervert." Humbert discovers Quilty's identity only near the end of his life, but his text points to Quilty's existence almost from the start of the narration. As he admits, clues are inserted "into the pattern of branches that I have woven throughout this memoir with the express purpose of hav-

LOLITA

ing the ripe fruit fall at the right moment" (274).
The first glimpse occurs in an apparently inconsequential listing of Humbert's jail-cell books.
Among them is *Who's Who in the Limelight* with the
listing, "Quilty, Clare, American Dramatist. . . ."
(33). The other clues will be found by an alert
reader. Their locations reveal the ways in which
the lives of Humbert and Quilty intersect as they
move toward their fatal convergence in Parking-
ton.

After Humbert finally unmasks Quilty, he kills
from the conviction that Quilty had defiled his
purer love. In the grotesquely humorous murder
scene, whose slapstick orchestration actually
heightens the horror, Humbert reads from a prepared typescript before pulling the trigger.

> Because you took advantage of a sinner
> because you took advantage
> because you took
> because you took advantage of my
>   disadvantage . . .
> because of all you did
> because of all I did not
> you have to die (301–02).

He will never acknowledge that Quilty is his dark
side, an alter ego parody, so that the murder is in
effect an attack upon himself. As he and Quilty roll

about the floor of Pavor Manor tussling for possession of Chum the gun, they appear indistinguishable from one another ("I rolled over him. We rolled over me. They rolled over him. We rolled over us" (301)). Driving away from the gory corpse, Humbert notes, "I was all covered with Quilty" (308).

In the interstices of Humbert's tale the reader is asked to recognize what Humbert does not—an independent version of Lolita different from Humbert's solipsized perception of her. Because the reader does not carry the blinders that restrict Humbert's view, the reader's Lolita will be not only the "beautiful hardly formed young girl whom modern co-education, juvenile mores, the campfire racket, and so forth had utterly and hopelessly depraved" (135). She should emerge in her own right. This other reality is glimpsed, for example, in a moment of voyeurism as Humbert observes Lolita at play. "Her tennis was the highest point to which I can imagine a young creature bringing the art of make-believe, although I daresay, for her it was the very geometry of basic reality" (233). Humbert does not understand that the description which follows discloses Lolita's independent existence, and that he is unintentionally providing a concrete demonstration of her discreteness, not unlike the view of the teasingly unknowable Cincinnatus provided by the narrator of *Invitation to a Beheading*:

She would wait and relax for a bar or two of white-lined time before going into the act of serving . . . always at ease, always rather vague about the score, always cheerful as she so seldom was in the dark life she led at home. . . . .[she] had a way of raising her bent left knee at the ample and springy start of the service cycle when there would develop and hang in the sun for a second a vital web of balance between toed foot, pristine armpit, burnished arm and far back-flung racket, as she smiled up with gleaming teeth at the small globe suspended so high in the zenith of the powerful and graceful cosmos she had created. . . . It had, that serve of hers, beauty, directness, youth" (233–34).

When Humbert encounters the pregnant seventeen-year old Dolly Schiller after a separation of several years, he understands, much too late, that his love has grown beyond the obsession for a prepubescent female child.

There she was with her ruined looks and her adult, rope-veined narrow hands and her gooseflesh white arms, and her shallow ears, and her unkempt armpits, there she was (my Lolita!), hopelessly worn at seventeen . . . and I looked and looked at her, and knew as clearly as I know I am to die, that I loved her more than anything I had ever seen or imagined on earth, or hoped for anywhere else (279).

AMERICAN NOVELS

Her independence now established, he is finally forced to recognize that his love is not (and never had been) shared by her.

In her washed-out gray eyes, strangely spectacled, our poor romance was for a moment reflected, pondered upon, and dismissed like a dull party, like a rainy picnic to which only the dullest bores had come, like a humdrum exercise, like a bit of dry mud caking her childhood (274).

Only when she is irrevocably lost to him does he fully comprehend the tragic dimension of his crime. On the penultimate page of the novel the reader will note that as Humbert awaits the police he recollects a day shortly after Lolita's disappearance when he stood on the edge of another road and heard the sounds of children at play. At that time he had only vaguely understood "that the hopelessly poignant thing was not Lolita's absence from my side, but the absence of her voice from that concord" (309–11). Humbert's unredeemable crime is that he had robbed Lolita of her childhood. In exchange for what he can never replace, he offers to the future the story of his love. As he says, "I see nothing for the treatment of my misery but the melancholy and very local palliative of articulate art" (285). So that she can "live in the minds of later generations," as payment for his crime upon

LOLITA

her, he offers up his tale which does succeed in outliving them both. "I am thinking," he writes at the close, "of aurochs and angels, the secret of durable pigments, prophetic sonnets, the refuge of art. And this is the only immortality you and I may share, my Lolita" (311).

Termed "the most allusive and linguistically playful novel in English since *Ulysses* (1922) and *Finnegans Wake* (1939)"[6] *Lolita* contains a profusion of word games, parodies and literary allusions. Readers are ably served by Carl Proffer's *Keys to LOLITA* and Alfred Appel, Jr.'s *The Annotated LOLITA* to help in identifying and elucidating many of them. The allusions to more than sixty authors primarily from English and French literatures (Humbert is writing a comparative history of French literature for English-speaking students), ranging alphabetically from Alcott to Virgil, function for the most part as alternative perspectives and subtexts for the consideration of erudite Humbert's individualized tale. The reader must be alert to the ways in which Humbert compares and distinguishes his love within the romantic tradition to which he alludes as he constantly casts about for literary precedents. Edgar Allan Poe (himself the husband of a twelve-year-old child bride) is the author most frequently referred to ("Dr. Edgar H. Humbert" is Humbert's alias at the Enchanted

Hunters). Taking the range of Poe allusions as but one example, the reader is asked to consider Humbert's nympholepsy in the context of Poe's poems, "Annabel Lee," "Lenore," and "The Raven"; Humbert's pursuit of Quilty in light of Poe's tales of ratiocination; the relationship between Humbert and Quilty from the perspective of Poe's uses of the double theme; and Humbert's fatal attraction to nymphets in view of Poe's philosophy of Beauty.

Because of Humbert's extensive detailing of the American setting, *Lolita* is considered the most American of Nabokov's novels. While Vladimir Nabokov reminds the reader of what cannot be condoned in the name of love, Humbert creates the story of a great passion and clothes it in 1950s American garb. From his Old World perspective, the enlightened European confronting the New World, the view appears jaundiced. Vladimir Nabokov came to know and love his adopted American homeland on cross-country summer trips in pursuit of butterfly specimens. Humbert's cross-country jaunts are colored by his obsession, his frantic search for Lolita's abductor, and his despair. His discerning eye offers an America observed from a troubled perspective.

We passed and re-passed through the whole gamut of American roadside restaurants, from the lowly Eat

LOLITA

with its deer head (dark trace of long tear at inner canthus), 'humorous' picture post cards of the posterior 'Kurort' type, impaled guest checks, life savers, sunglasses, adman visions of celestial sundaes, one half of a chocolate cake under glass, and several horribly experienced flies zigzagging over the sticky sugarpour on the ignoble counter; and all the way to the expensive place with the subdued lights, preposterously poor table linen, inept waiters (ex-convicts or college boys), the roan back of a screen actress, the sable eyebrows of her male of the moment, and an orchestra of zoot-suiters with trumpets (157).

Such descriptions reveal more about Humbert than about America. Teenage mores, progressive education, scenic drives, Hollywood westerns, motels and roadside restaurants startle Humbert and serve as targets of his cynical wit, but also as barometers of his state of mind. By and large the poshlust which is detailed is of the innocuous sort. "Nothing is more exhilarating," Nabokov wrote, "than philistine vulgarity" (317). And, he adds, "it had taken me some forty years to invent Russia and Western Europe, and now I was faced by the task of inventing America" (314). But do not confuse Humbert with Nabokov. At the end of his tale, Humbert recognizes that his observations of the American landscape have been distorted by the prism of his obsession: "We had been everywhere. We had really seen nothing. And I catch myself thinking today that our long journey had only defiled with a sinuous trail of slime the lovely, trustful, dreamy, enormous country" (177–78).

While declaring that he had been "forced to abandon my natural idiom, my untrammeled, rich, and infinitely docile Russian tongue for a second-rate brand of English" (318–319), Nabokov also wrote, "an American critic suggested that *Lolita* was the record of my love affair with the romantic novel. The substitution 'English language' for 'romantic novel' would make this elegant formula more correct" (318). *Lolita* offers a lavish display of Nabokov's stylistic talents—a wide array of alliteration and assonance, humorous rhymes ("welcome, fellow, to this bordello"), puns and word play of every sort ("a halter with too little to halt"), a vast lexical range (advertising jargon, dialect words, teenage slang, Gallicisms), a variety of neologisms ("gagoon," "libidream," "honeymonsoon"), and a symphony of rhythmic prose. This all combines with the highest levels of Nabokov's evocative abilities.

Beyond the tilled plain, beyond the toy roofs, there would be a slow suffusion of inutile loveliness, a low sun in a platinum haze with a warm, peeled-peach tinge pervading the upper edge of a two-dimensional, dove-gray cloud fusing with the distant amorous mist.

PNIN

There might be a line of spaced trees silhouetted
against the horizon, and hot still noons above a wil-
derness of clover, and Claude Lorrain clouds inscribed
remotely into misty azure with only their cumulus
part conspicuous against the neutral swoom of the
background. Or again, it might be a stern El Greco
horizon, pregnant with inky rain, and a passing
glimpse of some mummy-necked farmer, and all
around alternating strips of quick-silverish water and
harsh green corn, the whole arrangement opening like
a fan, somewhere in Kansas (154–55).

At one point Humbert remarks with rare perception that his attraction to nymphets had less to
do with their forbidden beauty than with "the
security of a situation where infinite perfections fill
the gap between the little given and the great
promised—the great rosegray never-to-be-had"
(266). As he discovers, that "gap" is not closed by
his tragic violation of Lolita, but it is filled by the
magical transformative powers of Nabokov's verbal art.

Pnin

For many readers *Pnin* (1957) is the warmest
and most accessible of Nabokov's novels. This is
due in part to the endearing portrait of its "weird,
funny, heartbreaking" hero, Professor Timofey

AMERICAN NOVELS

Pnin, and to the jocular treatment of American academia.[7] In part it is due to the impression that the text is straightforward and transparent. Because four chapters were first published as separate short stories in the *New Yorker* some readers consider *Pnin* a loosely joined series of vignettes which, as a whole, seem happily devoid of those perplexing narrative and thematic intricacies so typical of Nabokov's fictions.[8]

Actually, though, the careful reader will discover that *Pnin* is no less intricately structured or unified than any other Nabokov novel. Once again it is the method of narration which deserves initial scrutiny by the reader.

Though the point of view is ostensibly third person omniscient, the narrator is actually an active participant in the narrative. He is an acquaintance of Pnin's, and his claims to omniscience are questionable. Early in the text the narrator remarks—ironically, it turns out—"I do not know if it has ever been noted before that one of the main characteristics of life is discreteness."[9] He then ignores this important truth by proceeding to violate Pnin's discreteness with a narration based on the impossible assumption that Pnin's thoughts and feelings are known to him and that he is able to present and discuss them with full objectivity.

PNIN

But the narrator is only one of several persons who attempt to fictionalize Pnin's existence.

The discrepancy between the events narrated in the opening and closing of the novel emphasize the need to carefully consider the narrative point of view. In the opening, the narrator relates Pnin's misadventures while traveling to the Cremona Women's Club. He tells us that Pnin has taken the wrong train and is carrying in his jacket pocket Betty's term paper rather than the text of his lecture. Pnin, the reader is told, is able to retrieve his baggage, find the lecture notes, and then address the women of Cremona with talk in hand. In the closing lines of the novel, Jack Cockerell, the locally renowned imitator of Pnin and collector of Pnin-lore, tells a different story: "I am going to tell you the story of Pnin rising to address the Cremona Women's Club and discovering he had brought the wrong lecture" (190).

Bald, diminutive Timofey Pnin, "stunned by thirty-five years of homelessness" (143), is the quintessential exile. A full chronological portrait of his life, consisting largely of a series of losses, can be assembled by the reader through the careful piecing together of present-time events and a complex series of flashbacks. Of particular note are Pnin's intermittent seizures, not unlike heart attacks, which evoke important memories of previ-

AMERICAN NOVELS

ous "occasions of discomfort and despair" (21). The unrolling record of his accumulation of nearly intolerable losses ("the history of man is the history of pain!" (167))—native country, native culture, native language, parents, first love, wife, and, finally, job—which were precipitated by fate, circumstance, and the predation of others is saved, ultimately, from becoming excessively pathetic or sentimental by a narrative tone that is often light and humorous and because Pnin, the arch victim, finally proves victorious and whole, free of the encroachment of others.

"How should we diagnose his sad case?" the narrator muses rhetorically at the outset, informing the reader that Pnin's life in America was "a constant war with insensate objects that fell apart or attacked him. . . . Electric devices enchanted him. Plastics swept him off his feet. He had a deep admiration for the zipper" (13). Laughable, vulnerable, sad Pnin. The English language, in particular, presents "a special danger." His funny broken-English ("I haf nofing. I haf nofing left, nofing, nofing!" (61)) complements the image of his vulnerability. But the observant reader should note that Pnin's visit to "The Pines," in Chapter Five, casts him in a totally un-Pninian light. There, in the Russian émigré milieu which is his natural element and where he is no longer a displaced person, Pnin appears neither humorous nor inept. He is transformed into the most adroit croquet player, a man fluent in the social graces and eloquent in the use of the Russian language.

By employing a strategy not unlike that employed in the narrative of *Despair*, the author provides a series of associational cross-references duly recorded (but not understood) by the narrator, which allow the reader independent access to Pnin's "true" story. The most important of these is a profusion of references to squirrels and to Cinderella. Charles Nicol has demonstrated conclusively that the squirrel motif which runs conspicuously throughout the text provides the key to the novel.[10] The stuffed squirrel and squirrel-adorned wallpaper of his childhood; the squirrels which frequently eat nearby; the squirrel to whom the weeping Pnin gives a drink; the prized image of students who have seen Pnin taking his catalogue drawer "like a big nut, to a secluded corner and there make a quiet mental meal of it" (76); the girl Pnin loved in 1918, whom he had taught himself not to remember because he could not bear to live in a world in which her brutal death in a Nazi extermination camp was possible, was Mira Belochkin, a name which derives from (*belka*), the Russian word for "squirrel"—these and other

AMERICAN NOVELS

squirrel references linked to Pnin combine to form a major motif in his life and in this fiction.

The meaning of the association between Pnin and squirrel is revealed in a seemingly inconsequential bit of dialogue in Chapter Six. While admiring the glass bowl which Victor has given Pnin, Margaret Thayer remarks that she imagined Cinderella's glass shoes to be of the same color. But Pnin explains that Cinderella's shoes were not made of glass but of Russian squirrel fur. "It was, he said, an obvious case of the survival of the fittest among words, *verre* being more evocative than *vair* which, he submitted, came not from *varius*, variegated, but from *veveritsa*, Slavic for a certain beautiful, pale, winter-squirrel fur" (157). This odd footnote to the Cinderella tale, unearthed by Pnin's seemingly esoteric research on a *Petite Histoire* of Russian culture and repeated by the narrator who has no idea of its consequence, provides the reader with a clarification of the Pnin-squirrel association and serves as well as a sterling justification for the accumulation of factual details which form the body of Pnin's research.

The key lies in the relationship between Pnin and Victor, Pnin's ex-wife Liza's son by Eric Wind. Victor feels no kinship with his biological father. At the beginning of Chapter Four, the central chapter of the novel, Victor dreams about The King, "his more plausible father," pacing on a beach. By remarkable coincidence, at the end of the same chapter while Victor is visiting Pnin, Pnin has a dream in which he himself appears pacing on a beach. Pnin sends Victor a picture postcard representing the Gray Squirrel, and Victor, the fourteen-year-old prodigal artist who has learned to distinguish spectrum colors which grade into "Cinderella shades transcending human perception" (95), sends Pnin a glass bowl which he has made.

Margaret Thayer's remark and Pnin's explanation of the Cinderella story development provide an explanation for the Pnin-squirrel/Cinderella-glass linked patterning. The reader can see that its function is to allow the transformation (Cinderella is a tale of magical transformation) of Pnin into Victor's true father in every respect other than the biological. The squirrel-Pnin pattern is supplied by the author, not the narrator, for the reader's benefit, while naturally Pnin himself remains unaware of it. The emergence of the glass bowl, Victor's gift to Pnin, from the sink's sudsy water, intact despite the plunging and resonating nut-cracker—to the general surprise of Pnin and the narrator—proves Pnin victorious. It is the reader, grown accustomed to seeing Pnin as victim, who is likely to be most surprised when the bowl surfaces unbroken. The reader has come to expect the worst, and thus in a sense to create the worst. The unbroken bowl affirms Pnin's independence from all who would do him harm.

Pnin ultimately challenges the narrator's reliability in the final pages of the novel by remarking "Now, don't believe a word he says. He makes up everything. He once invented that we were schoolmates in Russia and cribbed at examinations. He is a dreadful inventor" (183). At this late moment in the novel the reader also learns that the narrator first saw Pnin in Russia; that Liza had married Pnin on the rebound from a broken affair with the narrator and had subsequently confessed the affair to her new husband; and that the narrator had only infrequently been in Pnin's company. Since Pnin knows that the narrator had been his wife's lover, it is not at all surprising that he firmly refuses to accept the narrator's request that Pnin remain at Waindell under his direction. "I will never work under him," (168) Pnin declares without a moment's hesitation. But he remains unaware that he has become a character in the narrator's fiction.

The information revealed in Chapter Seven challenges the accuracy of the narrative and obliges the reader to reread the novel, weighing each of the narrator's conclusions and opinions in light of the narrator's personal role in the lives of Pnin and

PNIN

Liza. These disclosures also pose another problem because there are specific details in the text which suggest that the never-named narrator and the author, Vladimir Nabokov, may be the same person. During Pnin's party the slightly inebriated Joan Clements remarks: " 'But don't you think—haw—that what he is trying to do—haw—practically in all his novels—haw—is—haw—to express the fantastic recurrence of certain situations?' " (158). The person referred to is not named. However the "compatriot" who replaces Pnin on the faculty is referred to as "a prominent Anglo-Russian writer who, if necessary, could teach all the courses that Pnin must keep in order to survive" (138). If indeed the narrator is the author, then the conclusion of the novel is one of the most remarkable in fiction. Having received Pnin's letter refusing under any circumstances to work for him, the narrator hastens to visit with Pnin on the morning following his arrival at Waindell. He is too late and the final glimpse that he (and the reader) gets of Pnin is the sight of the automobile carrying Timofey, "free at last," into the receding distance "where there was no saying that miracle might happen" (190). If narrator and author are the same person, then a fictional character has just escaped, impossibly, from the control of his creator and Pnin's victory is absolutely total.

AMERICAN NOVELS

Pale Fire

Pale Fire (1962) consists of a foreword, a 999-line poem, cancelled variant verses, 228 pages of commentary, and an index. It is likely be the most unconventional novel the reader has ever encountered. But its form is not without precedent. For one thing it is similar to Nabokov's rendition of Pushkin's *Eugene Onegin* (which has an introduction, Nabokov's translation of Pushkin's text, three volumes of notations, and an index), and as such Nabokov's novel serves as a commentary on his own and others' scholarly efforts. The violation of the standard form of the novel is also very much in the tradition of Russian literature. Pushkin's unconventional novel in verse, Turgenev's and Dostoevsky's novellas presented as "Notes" and "Diaries," and Tolstoy's *War and Peace*, in which historical fiction intermingles with nonfiction essays, are all examples of Russian writers' disregard for standard concepts of genre.

According to Mary McCarthy, in her illustrious review of the novel, *Pale Fire* is "a Jack-in-the-box, a Fabergé gem, a clockwork toy, a chess problem, an infernal machine, a trap to catch reviewers, a cat-and-mouse game, a do-it-yourself novel."[11] It is, in brief, a labyrinth whose unconventional form precludes a direct linear experiences of the text. The reader is obliged to work back and forth, cross-referencing, moving regularly from the commentary and index to the poem. This laborious process will result in the discovery of what McCarthy called "a creation of perfect beauty, symmetry, strangeness, originality, and moral truth . . . one of the very great works of art of this century."[12]

Pale Fire explores a complex of conflicting commentaries on the same events, with characters, author, and reader devising their own truths. The reader's first priority will be the attempt to untangle the novel's potential stories. John Shade, American, a sixty-one-year old teacher at Wordsmith College in New Wye, Appalachia, is the author of "Pale Fire," a poem in four cantos, consisting of 999 lines in heroic couplets. The poem makes reference to his various memories and offers his ruminations on consciousness, God, the Admirable butterfly, his wife and daughter, art, death, immortality, and beauty. On the morning of July 21, 1959, John Shade is murdered by a person who calls himself Jack Grey. Charles Kinbote, a colleague and Shade's next door neighbor, a non-American, bachelor and homosexual, procures the manuscript of the completed but as yet unpublished poem. He removes himself to a cabin in remote Cedarn, Utana, in order to edit the poem

AMERICAN NOVELS

for publication. The book before the reader is Kinbote's completed work.

As "an intimate friend of Shade, his literary adviser, editor and commentator,"[13] Kinbote offers the first level of interpretation of the poem, the poet, and the poet's death in his foreword, commentary and index ("Let me state that without my notes Shade's text simply has no human reality at all" (28). Kinbote affirms that John Shade was "a very dear friend" and that "Pale Fire," though seeming to be about Shade's life, is in reality a poem inspired by his own (Kinbote's) life. In the commentary Kinbote divulges his true identity as the exiled Charles II (Charles the Beloved) of Zembla, a distant northern country, who had been forced by revolution to abandon his throne and flee his homeland. Following protracted travels and with the aid of a friendly trustee he eventually procured a position at Wordsmith College. There he rented a house next to the Shades' residence, found numerous opportunities to share with Shade a great many tales of Zemblan life and the sad plight of its king, and became the poet's close friend in the hope that Shade would immortalize him in a poem. As he says, "I felt sure . . . that he would recreate in a poem the dazzling Zembla burning in my brain. I mesmerized him with it, I saturated him with my vision" (80). Meanwhile,

PALE FIRE

the king's enemies had hired an assassin, Jakob
Gradus, and as Shade proceeded to write "Pale
Fire," Gradus was drawing ever nearer to New
Wye. On July 21, the day on which Shade finished
writing his poem, Gradus arrived in New Wye
and, according to Kinbote, mistakenly killed Shade
while aiming his gun at him, Charles the Beloved.
Taken into custody but disguising his true identity,
the murderer claimed to be Jack Grey, a lunatic.[14]
Kinbote then absconded with the manuscript, he
explains, because "one's attachment to a masterpiece may be utterly overwhelming, especially
when it is the underside of the weave that entrances the beholder and only begetter, whose own
past intercoils there with the fate of the innocent
author" (17).

Pale Fire focuses on the divergent realities
represented by the two central "fictions" in the
text, both of which are commentaries—Shade's
poem, which is his commentary on his life, and
Kinbote's commentary on the poem and on Shade.
Both are "readings" of reality. In the former, the
reader (Shade) approaches the text and his life with
the free consciousness of a poet; in the latter
instance the reader (Kinbote) approaches the text
and life (Shade's and his own) with preconceptions
that force the material into a prefabricated pattern
(Zembla and its King). The reader of *Pale Fire*, in

turn, supplies yet another text created from his or her reading of, or commentary on, the entire novel. The "correctness" of that reading, i.e. any understanding of the text, will depend upon the reader's ability to locate, unravel and then elucidate the overall patterning which has been provided by the author. The task is difficult, but then it is Nabokov's conviction that conscious reading (like conscious life) is a demanding affair.

The attentive reader working his way through Kinbote's annotations to the poem will be bothered by the tenuous linkages between the commentary and the verse. Kinbote's inferences and conclusions will appear to be irrelevant because Zemblan lore and the King's life would appear to have little if anything to do with the actual text of the poem. Kinbote uses the thinnest excuse to relate his own story. Thus the phrase, "a great conspiracy," (from "a great conspiracy of books," line 171) serves as the pretext for Kinbote's narrative on the selection of Gradus as assassin, and the phrase, "A jet's pink trail above the sunset fire" (line 286) sets off a lengthy description of Gradus' travels. At best, only a few of Kinbote's annotations may be relevant not to the poem, but to cancelled lines of the text which Kinbote claims Shade wrote but which no one else has seen.

The reader should have little difficulty con-

PALE FIRE

cluding that "Pale Fire," contrary to Kinbote's assertions, is not about King Charles and Zembla. Evidence is found in the commentary that Shade was not Kinbote's good friend, that Shade and Kinbote seldom met, and that the composition of the poem was not influenced by Kinbote. The death of Shade also has another explanation. The reader is told in the preface that Kinbote's rented house was owned by Judge Goldsworth, and later information reveals that Jack Grey was a lunatic who had escaped from the State Asylum for the Insane in order to seek revenge on Judge Goldsworth, the man who had put him there. He shot Shade because he confused him with Goldsworth. "Pale Fire" will remain John Shade's highly personal and autobiographical poem, while Kinbote emerges as a madman who has projected his individual mania (the fantasy worlds of Zembla and its King) on Shade's life and work. Writing in an isolated cabin where he must rely entirely on memory, frequently failing to provide accurate notations because he lacks access to any libraries, Kinbote becomes a parody of the worst kind of scholar.

Alternate realities are once again Nabokov's subject. Kinbote correctly affirms that " 'reality' is neither the subject nor the object of true art which creates its own special reality having nothing in

common with the average 'reality' perceived by the
communal eye" (130). Yet in his commentary he
has attempted, impossibly, to create from John
Shade's poem (which is in itself a uniquely imagined reality) another "artistic" reality of his own.
One man has taken another man's art for his own
personal reality. And that, as Nabokov always
maintained, is unpardonable.

This complex question of separate realities can
be taken a step further if the reader doubts the
separate identities of Shade and Kinbote, and proposes the existence of a primary author (other than
Nabokov). One reading of the novel argues that
Kinbote has created the entire text. "Gradus and
Shade are as much figments of Kinbote's imagination as Charles the Beloved and the far-distant land
of Zembla."[15] Another view proposes that the
primary author of the work is John Shade and that
Kinbote, King Charles, and Zembla are his creations. "A sane man may invent an insane character, and we call him an artist; an insane man who
invents a perfectly sane character is also an artist,
but *ipso facto* no longer insane in the way that
Kinbote is. What sort of an Alice would the Mad
Hatter make for us?" In this view, Kinbote could
not be the primary author for then *Pale Fire* would
be nothing more than a pointless "description of a
rare type of madness."[16] A third reading argues

PALE FIRE

that *both* Kinbote and Shade are the creations of Dr. V. Botkin. D. Barton Johnson studies the text and index and argues that (1) the author of the index is mad Kinbote (not Shade); (2) many of the entries are gratuitous asides with no relation to the text; (3) the entries demonstrate conclusively that Kinbote and Shade are separate individuals and (4) careful analysis of clues planted in the index, particularly the omission of persons who should be there, reveals that V. Botkin, an "American scholar of Russian descent," is the actual primary author of the work. Botkin, another professor at Wordsmith, is, according to Johnson, a schizophrenic who "is writing a novel about the entirely fictional characters Kinbote, Shade, and Gradus" and "in his guise as Kinbote, is the protagonist, the editor, and the narrator." Because "V. Botkin" stands anagrammatically close to "V. Nabokov," closer than does Shade or Kinbote, Botkin, says Johnson, can be considered the author-persona in the novel who is pointing to the ultimate author, V. Nabokov.[17]

Mary McCarthy's observation that *Pale Fire* is an infernal do-it-yourself novel is well taken. The unconventional form obliges the reader to unravel and isolate its constituent parts (story, identity of the narrator, identity of the characters, relationships among them) and then recombine them before arriving at any comprehension of the whole. The final step, of course, is to identify the larger, superimposed patterns provided by the author, Nabokov. His presence in the work is manifested in various ways. To cite but one example, in Canto I, lines 139–156, Shade describes "a thread of subtle pain, tugged at by playful death" which ran through him one day at age eleven as he lay on the floor and watched "a tin wheelbarrow pushed by a tin boy." The poem ends with the image repeated, "Some neighbor's gardener, I guess—goes by/ Trundling an empty barrow up the lane" (lines 998–99). The repetition of the wheelbarrow image leaves the association with "playful death" unstated but understood. What Shade does not and could not know, is that he will die on the very day he writes the lines, thus prefiguring his own death. This perfect example of life imitating art reveals the author's hand.

The poem, "Pale Fire," is the work of a talented poet. Canto I holds Shade's recollections of his childhood and his first intimations of mortality; Canto II is centered in the life and death of his daughter; Canto III presents the poet's meditations on death and the hereafter; Canto IV bespeaks the life of the poet and the man. The commentary offered by Kinbote provides some useful information about Shade's life, but the bulk of the exegesis,

as already noted, must be handled with care. By
and large Kinbote's commentary helps to clarify
not the similarities but the differences which exist
between the poet and the critic. Kinbote is a
Christian, Shade is not ("My God died young.
Theolatry I found/Degrading, and its premises,
unsound./No free man needs a God" (lines
99–101)). Kinbote has a theological justification for
suicide; Shade has a passion for life. Kinbote is a
poor naturalist; Shade's parents were ornitholo-
gists and the Admirable butterfly serves as the
emblem of his love. Kinbote strives to establish the
semblances of his life in Shade's art; Shade is not
interested in semblances, only differences ("Re-
semblances are the shadows of differences. Different people see different similarities and similar
differences" (265). Most importantly Kinbote has
only the enclosed, fabricated, fantasy kingdom of
Zembla. Shade has an active consciousness, a
father's grief, the love for his wife, the poet's gift,
and his mortal conviction that there is a greater
reality, "a contrapuntal theme."

> Just this: not text, but texture; not the dream
> But topsy-turvical coincidence,
> Not flimsy nonsense, but a web of sense.
> Yes! It sufficed that I in life could find
> Some kind of link-and-bobolink, some kind
> Of correlated pattern in the game,

AMERICAN NOVELS

> Plexed artistry, and something of the same
> Pleasure in it as they who played it found.
> It did not matter who they were (lines 810–815).

Kinbote never divulges, in commentary or index, the location of the stolen crown jewels of fantasy-Zembla. But the reader is meant to find jewels where Nabokov's poet, John Shade, has secreted them—in the "diamonds of frost" (line 19), "jade leaves" (line 50), "opal cloudlet" (line 119), "emerald egg case" (line 238) and "topaz of dawn" (line 881) of "Terra the Fair, an orbicle of jasp" (558).

At the close of his commentary, Kinbote suggests the origin of the poem's title in the following remark: "My commentary to this poem . . . represents an attempt to sort out those echoes and wavelets of fire, and pale phosphorescent hints, and all the many subliminal debts to me" (297). Actually Shade's poem borrows its title from Shakespeare's *Timon of Athens*, IV, iii.

> The sun's a thief, and with his great attraction
> Robs the vast sea: the moon's an arrant thief,
> And her pale fire she snatches from the sun:

This is susceptible to readings other than the misrepresentation of the lines given by Kinbote in his commentary (79–80). In simplest terms it could be an expression of the poet's honest modesty. More likely, it could be understood to mean that while the sun by its radiance robs the sea, the water it takes will inevitably return to bathe the land. The moon, however, remains a vagrant and shameless thief who steals its pale radiance from the sun and gives nothing back in return. In this there is a telling commentary on the place of the poet (Shade) and the critic (Kinbote).

The opening of "Pale Fire" reads:

> I was the shadow of the waxwing slain
> By the false azure in the windowpane
> I was the smudge of ashen fluff

Kinbote glosses these lines with the following comment: "The image in these opening lines evidently refers to a bird knocking itself out, in full flight, against the outer surface of a glass pane in which a mirrored sky, with its slightly darker tint and slightly slower cloud, presents the illusion of continued space" (73). He obviously misses the point. It is the critic who perishes when he mistakes the reflection for the reality. The poet remains the shadow, the "ashen fluff," who "lived on, flew on, in the reflected sky" (lines 3–4).

Ada

In many respects *Ada or Ardor: A Family Chronicle* is the apogee of Nabokov's art. As his longest, most complex, most ambitious, and most open-ended work, it has drawn a wide range of reader response and interpretation. Nabokov called it his "most cosmopolitan and poetic" novel,[18] while the *New York Times* designated it "the most widely unread best-seller" of 1969.[19] It has been hailed as "a great work of art, a necessary book, radiant and rapturous, affirming the power of love and imagination,"[20] and it has also been termed a flawed masterpiece, or even "a disaster—overblown, overwritten."[21] The reader is advised to approach *Ada* in the same way he approaches any Nabokov novel—ready to consider questions of point of view, to identify thematic patterns, to isolate and distinguish alternate realities. Since *Ada* is the most lavishly and intricately detailed of Nabokov's novels, presenting the most fully embodied of his many fictional worlds, the reader will find the process especially demanding.

Opening *Ada* one first encounters a two-page genealogical chart. The first line of the text ("All happy families are more or less dissimilar; all unhappy ones are more or less alike") is an inversion of the famous first line of Tolstoy's *Anna Karenina* ("All happy families resemble one another, but each unhappy family is unhappy in its own way"). This is followed by an erroneous reference to yet another book by Tolstoy. The remaining paragraphs of Part I, Chapter One, begin to fill out the genealogical chart in a profusion of names, dates, places and events. The names are strange; the places mentioned are unrecognizable; the chronology of dates and events is complicated. Parenthetic remarks abound and the language of the chapter is difficult (tesselated, cicerone, ectoplasmic, granoblastically). The experienced Nabokov reader, attuned to the importance of remembering and controlling the details of Nabokov's fictions, will be challenged. Some readers will read no further. Yet, once past Chapter Three the narrative assumes a more leisurely pace as Van sets about describing Ardis Hall, his discovery of Ada, and the growth of their passion.

Ada is in the form of an autobiography. Its author, Ivan (Van) Veen, gazing backwards, is 87 years old when the writing begins and 97 years old when the book is completed. The novel is structured in five unequal parts, each part getting progressively shorter as the text moves into the present time of the writing. Van's primary subject is his love for Ada. But since he is a philosopher, a psychologist, a novelist and a sexual athlete, the memoirs also concern his activities and thoughts in each of these realms. Part 1, larger than the other four parts together, has forty-three chapters which begin with his family genealogy and center on the genesis, flowering, and power of his "passionate, hopeless, rapturous sunset love."[22] Looking seventy-three years back into his past, Van concentrates on his memories of two summers spent in the arbors and ardors of Ardis. In 1884, when he was fourteen and Ada was twelve, their love was sexually consecrated on The Night of the Burning Barn. After a four-year separation with only two brief interludes, Van is reunited with Ada at Ardis in the summer of 1888, a less happy time as he learns of her several infidelities. Part 2 recounts Van's activities during the next period of separation which ends four years later in 1892 when they are reunited in the hope of a long future together. This hope is shattered on February 5, 1893, when their father learns of their incestuous relationship and urges them to cease seeing each other. Part 3 covers events during the period 1893–1922—Ada married to Andrey Vinelander, Van separating from her for seventeen years, the deaths of their mother (Marina), father (Demon), and half-sister (Lucette), and the end of the lover's separation. Part 4, twenty-eight pages in length, recounts two days in mid-July 1922 and centers on Van's work on his book, *The Texture of Time*. The six chapters of part 5 find Van and Ada together on his ninety-seventh birthday in 1967 with his memoir nearly completed.

ADA

Nabokov tells us that *Ada* was originally composed on approximately 2,500 3 × 5 index cards and "caused more trouble than all my other novels."[23] It might be appropriate to imagine that Nabokov shuffled those index cards before typing out the full manuscript. The text has a full share of riddles, fatidic dates, repetitive details, word puzzles, puzzling words and puzzling asides complementing the basic story lines. This most elaborate of Nabokov's novels presents a prefigured fictional world which comes closest to reproducing the complex, deceptive, multi-layered dimensions that Nabokov finds in "reality." Proceeding from his avowed belief that any reality can always be peeled back to reveal successive layers of meaning, while remaining ultimately unknown, the reader would be wise to approach this novel in that spirit. *Ada* is the least likely of any of Nabokov's novel to lend itself to simple paraphrase or all-encompassing reductive interpretations. More than any other, it remains an open book which rewards the reader with each successive reading.

The reader's understanding of *Ada* will depend in large part on his or her conclusions concerning the reliability of Van's narration and the function of the central theme of incest. Determining the reliability of the narration is not a simple matter. For one thing, the novel has more than the usual complexities of autobiography. Van chooses to recount his memoirs not in the first person, but in the third-person mode which implies indisputable authorial omniscience and objectivity. But there are other narrative voices. Ada provides marginal notes, oral corrections, and annotations to the text which sometimes question the accuracy of Van's memory and commentary. Ronald Oranger, who edits the text, occasionally inserts his own comments, and Violet Knox, who types the text, makes several errors and changes in the process. One effect of these many voices adding to or interrupting the narrative is a regular movement in the time perspective from the past recollected to the present moment of writing and editing, serving to remind the reader of the years which have elapsed and the pivotal role that memory plays in the narration.

The reader must take into account Van's character, his motivation(s) for writing, the accuracy of his recall, and the degree to which his imagination appears to alter the facts. He claims that his memoir is "ninety-seven percent true, and three percent likely."[24] Unlike Hermann, Humbert, or Kinbote, Van is assuredly neither totally or partially insane, though at the age of ninety-seven he may be somewhat senile. He is a talented, well-read, and practiced writer—erudite and stylish. He has a more than generous amount of self-assuredness and ego, and his tale of love is tremendously compelling in its joy and intensity. Yet several conclusions concerning his reliability are possible, and each must of course be based upon the particulars of the narration. As Ada cautions Van, "the detail is all" (71).

On one hand, the reader can conclude that Van's testimony is dependable, undistorted, and holds no hidden motives. His tale might be accepted as "objective" fact, his life and narrative being exactly what they claim to be. Proceeding along these lines, the reader might also determine, because of similarities between Van's and Nabokov's views on time and art and similarities in their verbal dexterity and playfulness, that Van is identical to Nabokov. "Nabokov gave these characters [Van and Ada] a supreme uniqueness," one critic has written, "by giving them his own view of the world and of life."[25] However this conclusion seems to be refuted by Nabokov, who emphatically remarked, "I loathe Van Veen."[26] If Van is not to be trusted, then another possibility, as might be expected by a practiced reader of Nabokov's fiction, is to conclude that Van is one more of Nabokov's unreliable narrators.

How the reader's solution to the question of Van's reliability will affect an understanding of the

AMERICAN NOVELS

text can be exemplified by considering the novel's setting. The reader is told that the action of the novel occurs in the world of Antiterra, also known as Demonia, while another, twinned world, Terra the Fair, is also thought by some to exist. Van is himself a "terrapist" and the author of a poor-selling philosophical novel, *Letters From Terra*. Nabokov termed the anachronistic world of his novel a "dream America." Its history and geography are entirely unfamiliar. Because the Tartars were not defeated in 1380, Russians were driven into North America and the events of the novel take place in what is called Amerussia. Alaska has become Russian Estoty, and there is also a French Estoty. The Commonwealth of Britain extends from "scoto-Scandinavia to the Riviera" and there is "Tartary, an independent inferno, which . . . spread[s] from the Baltic and Black Seas to the Pacific Ocean" (3–4). Place names are given in Russian, English, and French, the three languages of Antiterra's geography and people. In this world one finds the clepsydrophone, the petroloplane, the dorotelevision, the lammer (flying carpet), and the hydrogram, among other futuristic devices of communication and conveyance. While most of the events of the novel have nineteenth-century dates, Antiterra's nineteenth century also includes James Joyce, movies, and bikinis.

ADA

How the setting is understood will depend upon the reader's judgment of Van's reliability. If the reader decides to accept the narrative as objective fact, as some have done, then it is possible to conclude that Antiterra is "actual," a world of science fiction. Alfred Appel, for example, declares that "Antiterra's startling geographic boundaries are the result of Nabokov's unique version of the 'What *if*—?' mode of S[cience] F[iction]."[27] If the reader identifies Van Veen with Vladimir Nabokov he can then proceed to understand the fantasy of Antiterra as a sort of personal literary apotheosis in which Nabokov has created an intimate fantasy world which imaginatively embraces his own trilingual and tricultural biography. Van's story will thus become, in a sense, a parallel version of Nabokov's own memoirs.

If, however, the reader questions and finally doubts the reliability of Van's narration, Antiterra might then be seen as the personal fantasy of Van (and Ada). "The Past," Nabokov wrote, "is a constant accumulation of images, but our brain is not an ideal organ for constant retrospection and the best we can do is to pick out and try to retain those patches of rainbow light flitting through memory . . . The bad memoirist re-touches his past, and the result is a blue-tinted or pink-shaded photograph taken by a stranger to console sentimental bereavement.''[28] The reader who concludes that Van is a bad memoirist, based always upon careful consideration of details, will then try to distinguish between the fantasy world configured by the power of his memory and some other, more ''real'' world. The argument may be that Van's narrative is distorted by his forgetfulness and his confusing of various parallels between art and life, by the intrusion of dreams into his memory, by the creation of metaphorical inscapes, and by the distortion of details surrounding pivotal events in his life. Charles Nicol has followed this argument and concluded that ''to create normal order out of Van's disorder'' is the actual ''game'' and story of *Ada*.[29]

Sibling incest is the novel's central theme. Society believes that Van and Ada are cousins; they themselves maintain that they are half-brother and half-sister; but actually Van and Ada are full brother and sister. The genealogical tree that Van provides, designating him as the child of Demon and Aqua Veen, and Ada as the child of Daniel and Marina Veen, is in error. Van and Ada are both the offspring of a continuing affair between Demon Veen and Marina Durmanov. The corroborating details are found in those difficult to get through first chapters which present family history. The reader will most likely remain undisturbed by the

ADA

violation of this greatest social, moral, and ethical taboo, having once discovered its true nature. This will be due largely to the exuberance and brilliance with which Van narrates the story, leaving most readers spellbound by the "unique super-imperial couple" who share such a powerful love.

Understanding exactly how the incest theme functions in *Ada* should form the foundation for any general understanding of the novel. But since it is a work with a wide potential of realities, it follows that a variety of interpretations is possible. As a first matter, it should be apparent to the reader that the theme of incest is not employed as an excuse for prurience. Antiterra is a lusty place and many of its inhabitants avail themselves of the numerous delights offered by its Villa Venus Clubs. Ada has great physical needs, Van possesses remarkable potency, and the sexual core of their relationship raises questions concerning the basis and texture of their love and its effect upon others. But were Nabokov interested in titillation, he would be inexcusably guilty of missing far too many fine opportunities to exploit sexual situations. Incest in fact has other uses.

Since Nabokov maintained that the genealogy of a literary work is not "reality" but the literary tradition of which it is a part, it is possible to conclude that Nabokov's real interests in *Ada* are literary, rather than ethical or moral. Close analysis discloses that incestuous relationships may be discerned in several generations of the Zemski and Temnosiniy families, thus establishing Van's and Ada's love not as a unique phenomenon, but as part of a long family tradition of incestuous relationships. As he recounts his life, Van makes frequent use of allusions to Russian, French and English literature, primarily parodistically, and at various moments compares events in his life to similar events in "the Novel's Evolution in the History of Literature" (79). Moreover, the title of the novel reminds us that Van's memoir is a family chronicle, while the range of allusions, though broad, is for the most part to earlier literary treatments of incest (particularly by Chateaubriand and Byron) and to other family chronicles (particularly of the nineteenth century).[30] D. Barton Johnson, for one, argues that the novel is centrally "a parodistic reworking of the great Romantic theme of sibling incest," with incest serving as "a master metaphor for the creative intercourse of several generations of sibling incest novels in the three major literatures to which Nabokov's novel is heir."[31]

Other understandings of the incest theme focus upon the central role which Lucette, Van's and Ada's half-sister, plays in their lives. They are her

ADA

willful corrupters, allowing her to witness, and then encouraging her to enter into their sexual games. They tease and tantalize, and when she is unable to attain the one thing she desires—taking Ada's place in Van's bed—like Shakespeare's virginal Ophelia, she chooses a watery death. In a typically Nabokovian manner, a key passage occurs at the end of the novel. It raises questions that can only be solved by careful rereading. In the midst of a discussion between the elderly lovers regarding their own mortality, Ada suddenly exclaims:

'Oh, Van, oh Van, we did not love her enough. *That's* whom you should have married, the one sitting feet up, in balerina black, on the stone ballustrade, and then everything would have been all right—I would have stayed with you both in Ardis Hall, and instead of that happiness, handed out gratis, instead of all that we *teased* her to death!'

Was it time for the morphine? No, not yet. Time-and-pain had not been mentioned in the *Texture*. Pity, since an element of pure time enters into pain, into the thick, steady, solid duration of I-can't-bear-it pain; nothing gray-gauzy about it, solid as a black bole, I can't, oh. . . . (586–587).

Their lives nearly over and Van's written story of their love completed, Ada returns to her most troubling memory. Van's response to her lament is ambiguous because it is unclear whether the pain he is suffering is only physical, despite his remark several lines later, "Rather humiliating that physical pain makes one supremely indifferent to such moral issues as Lucette's fate" (587). In a perfectly apt manner, the novel which begins with a variant of the opening sentence of *Anna Karenina* closes with a variant to the closing of Anna's story in Tolstoy's novel. In that work the strong pains of a throbbing toothache commingle with the psychic pain of her lover's regrets, and it is unclear to the reader which is the more painful for Vronsky. Here the reader of *Ada* is left to wonder if at least part of Van's pain is actually from guilt, and if the true genesis of his story, controlling the way in which it is told, is the unspoken recognition of his unpardonable role in Lucette's death.

If the reader believes that Van's narration is unreliable, it can be argued that what it unsuccessfully hides is the real story of the novel—the tragic results of a love triangle composed of Van, Ada, and Lucette. Unable to escape the reality of Lucette and his feelings of guilt concerning his role in her death, Van, according to Bobbie Ann Mason, "tries to blame the disastrous consequences of his affair with his sister upon his heritage, upon his corrupt and luxurious family, and upon a demonic planet with narrow-minded conventions."[32] With Ada as his accomplice, he fabricates the world of Antiterra to serve as a justification for his actions. As he says to Ada, "I will . . . redeem our childhood by making a book of it: Ardis, a family chronicle" (406). Proof would come by locating contradictions, imprecisions, and obvious distortions in the details of his narrative. Van as the proud brachiambulant Mascodagama parading about on his hands, seeing the world from upside down and triumphing over "the Ardis of time," would be a fitting image. His ignorance of birds and butterflies, the realia of the natural world, would deserve consideration. Sibling incest will appear to function as an extreme metaphor for the limitations of solipsism and self-love, two frequent subjects in Nabokov's writings, and Van's tale would appear as an elaborate self-justification of actions for which he refuses responsibility.

If, however, careful rereading of the novel uncovers no clear evidence that Van actually feels remorse regarding Lucette, the reader can conclude that Van is not trying to hide anything because he never recognizes the consequences of his actions. He is honestly celebrating the uniqueness of his love and long life and is completely indifferent to the fate of Lucette. Nabokov, it can then be inferred, places Lucette at the center of the major motifs and interconnections of the work in

AMERICAN NOVELS

order to demonstrate for the *reader's* benefit the extent of Van's and Ada's "lack of concern for those they dismiss as immaterial to their own needs and wants."[33] *Ada* can then be understood, argues Brian Boyd, as "a study in the moral blindness that can accompany even the most exceptional intelligence and love."[34] Freedom and responsibility, the great themes of modern Russian literature from Pushkin and Lermontov through Tolstoy and Chekhov, become the main themes of *Ada*. Van is guilty of having failed to recognize the effect his brilliant and joyful love has had on others, failed to understand the "intimate interconnections between people's lives, interconnections which impose on human life all the obligations of moral responsibility."[35]

Ada is a challenging novel. However the reader chooses to understand it, the point of the elaborate and complex patterning and the problematic narrative form is not simply to engage in a devilish game. Nabokov's magical fictions always offer multiplicities of understanding and here, regardless of the interpretation the reader devises, it is certain, as Boyd has so aptly stated, that Nabokov with this novel "allows other worlds of wonderful possibility to surround the one we know" and that with each new reading Nabokov "encourages us to look for these new worlds by looking deeper into the reality of this [novel]."[36]

That it is difficult, if not impossible, to propose inclusive commentary for the novel has been playfully acknowledged by Nabokov himself in a most unusual manner. The later 1970 Penguin paperback edition of the text includes "Notes to Ada" by Vivian Darkbloom, a section not found in any American edition.[37] Nabokov's readers will recognize Darkbloom as a character from *Lolita* and as an anagram of "Vladimir Nabokov." Darkbloom's notes to the novel prove to be inadequate, inaccurate, unreliable and humorous. By adding to the literature of commentary in this unusual way, Nabokov has himself demonstrated the problems of constructing such commentary, while at the same time providing new materials for continuing interpretation.

Notes

1. For a summary of *Lolita*'s publishing history in America see F. W. Dupee, "*Lolita* in America," *Encounter* Feb. 1959:30–35. For the worldwide history see "Vladimir Nabokov: The Work of Art as Dirty Book" in Sally Dennison, *Alternative Literary Publishing: Five Modern Histories* (Iowa City, IA: University of Iowa Press, 1984).

2. Edmund White, "Nabokov: Beyond Parody," George Gibian and Stephen Jan Parker, eds., *The Achievements of Vladimir Nabokov*

AMERICAN NOVELS

(Ithaca, NY: Center for International Studies, Cornell University, 1984) 18.

3. Earl D. Sampson, "Postscript to the Russian Edition of *Lolita*," J. E. Rivers and Charles Nicol, eds. *Nabokov's Fifth Arc* (Austin, TX: University of Texas Press) 192. This is the English translation of Nabokov's postscript to his own Russian translation of *Lolita*; the text differs from the postscript to the original version.

4. Andrew Field infers thematic relationships with "A Nursery Tale" (1926), "A Dashing Fellow" (1930), "A Russian Beauty" (1934), and a story related by Zina's father in Chapter Three of *The Gift* (*Nabokov: His Life in Art* (Boston: Little, Brown, 1967) 325–35. The earliest extended treatment of nympholepsy is found in Nabokov's 1939 novella, *Volshebnik*. Though never published in Russian, the work has been rendered into English by Dmitri Nabokov under the title, *The Enchanter* (New York: G. P. Putman's Sons, 1986).

5. Vladimir Nabokov, "On a Book Entitled *Lolita*" in *Lolita* (New York: G. P. Putnam's Sons, 1958) 313.

6. Alfred Appel, Jr., ed. *The Annotated Lolita* (New York: McGraw-Hill, 1970) ix. Further references to *Lolita* and the author's afterword will be from this edition. Page numbers will be noted parenthetically.

7. From the back cover blurb to the Avon Library paperback edition of *Pnin* (1969): "A weird, funny heartbreaking hero indeed is Timofey Pnin. Pnin is the professor of Russian in an American college who takes the wrong train to deliver a lecture in a language he cannot master. . . ."

8. Chapters 1 ("Pnin"), 3 ("Pnin's Day"), 4 ("Victor Meets Pnin"), and 6 ("Pnin Gives a Party") were published separately in *The New Yorker*, 1953–55.

9. Vladimir Nabokov, *Pnin* (Garden City, NY: Doubleday, 1957) 19. Further references will be noted parenthetically.

10. Charles Nicol, "Pnin's History" *Novel* Spring 1971: 197–208; reprinted in Phyllis Roth, ed. *Critical Essays on Vladimir Nabokov* (Boston: G. K. Hall, 1984) 93–104.

11. Mary McCarthy, "A Bolt from the Blue," *The New Republic* 4 June 1962:21.

AMERICAN NOVELS

12. McCarthy, 27.

13. Vladimir Nabokov, *Pale Fire* (New York: G. P. Putnam's Sons, 1962) 28. Further references will be noted parenthetically.

14. For a detailed chronology of the novel see Kevin Pilon "A Chronology of *Pale Fire*," Carl Proffer, ed. *A Book of Things About Vladimir Nabokov* (Ann Arbor, MI: Ardis, 1974) 218–25.

15. Page Stegner, *The Art of Vladimir Nabokov: Escape Into Aesthetics* (New York: Dial Press, 1966) 129.

16. Andrew Field, *Nabokov: His Life in Art* (Boston: Little, Brown, 1967) 317.

17. D. Barton Johnson, *Worlds in Regression: Some Novels of Vladimir Nabokov* (Ann Arbor, MI: Ardis, 1985) 72.

18. Vladimir Nabokov, *Strong Opinions* (New York: McGraw-Hill, 1963) 179.

19. "Outstanding Books of the Year," *The New York Times Book Review* 7 Dec. 1969:90.

20. Alfred Appel, Jr., review of *Ada*, *The New York Times Book Review* 4 May 1969.

21. Morris Dickstein, "Nabokov's Folly," *The New Republic* 28 June 1969:27.

22. *Strong Opinions* 91.

23. *Strong Opinions* 138.

24. Vladimir Nabokov, *Ada or Ardor: A Family Chronicle* (New York: McGraw-Hill, 1969) 567. Further references will be noted parenthetically.

25. Donald Morton, *Vladimir Nabokov* (New York: Frederick Ungar, 1974) 135.

26. *Strong Opinions* 120.

27. Alfred Appel, Jr., "*Ada* Described," *Nabokov: Criticism, Reminiscences, Translations, and Tributes*, eds. Appel and Newman. (Evanston, IL: Northwestern University Press, 1970) 167.

28. *Strong Opinions* 186.

29. Charles Nicol, "Ada or Disorder," *Nabokov's Fifth Arc*, eds. Rivers and Nicol (Austin, TX: University of Texas Press, 1982) 231.

30. D. Barton Johnson, *Worlds in Regression: Some Novels of Vladimir Nabokov* (Ann Arbor, MI: Ardis, 1985) 132–33.

AMERICAN NOVELS

31. For a partial listing of allusions to Russian literature see Carl Proffer, "*Ada* as Wonderland: A Glossary of Allusions to Russian Literature," *A Book of Things About Vladimir Nabokov*, ed. Carl Proffer (Ann Arbor, MI: Ardis, 1974) 249–79.

32. Bobbie Ann Mason, *Nabokov's Garden. A Guide to ADA* (Ann Arbor, MI: Ardis, 1974) 13.

33. Brian Boyd, *Nabokov's ADA: The Place of Consciousness* (Ann Arbor, MI: Ardis, 1985) 94.

34. Boyd 93.

35. Boyd 104.

36. Boyd 212.

37. Darkbloom's "Notes," and notes to his "Notes" by J. E. Rivers and William Walker can be found in *Nabokov's Fifth Arc*, eds. Rivers and Nicol (Austin, TX: University of Texas Press, 1982) 242–95.

CHAPTER FOUR

Other Works

Vladimir Nabokov was a prolific writer. As novelist, short story author, poet, playwright, memoirist, scenarist, essayist, reviewer, literary scholar, lepidopterist, translator, and teacher he left an oeuvre which rivals in size the ninety volumes of the collected works of Leo Tolstoy. Even his interviews qualify as formal works. Preferring not to speak extemporaneously, he required interviewers to submit written questions to which he responded with carefully considered written replies. It is largely as a novelist that Nabokov earned his reputation as one of the greatest writers of the twentieth century, and thus to complete the consideration of his prose fiction, some mention, however brief, must be made of his other novels, the short stories, and two facets of his nonfiction writings which bear importantly upon the fiction.

OTHER WORKS

Novels

King, Queen, Knave (published 1928/translated into English 1968), the novel which followed *Mary*, is another reworking of the classic triangle (husband, wife, lover). But the characters are German, not Russian as in *Mary* and the subject is harlotry, not exile and first love. "Of all my novels this bright brute is the gayest," Nabokov declares in his introduction. "Expatriation, destitution, nostalgia had no effect on its elaborate and rapturous composition."[1] Played out with a deck of two-dimensional, cardlike figures, the novel is a grotesquely ribald tale of marital infidelity and unkind fate.

The Eye (1930/1965) is a short novella in which Nabokov for the first time utilizes first-person narration to explore the nature of solipsism. Following an unsuccessful attempt at suicide, the protagonist, Smurov, turns to a hyperconscious examination of himself and the images of himself projected in the views of others ("I do not exist: there exist but the thousands of mirrors that reflect me").[2] Unable to fix his self-image, he concludes that "the only happiness in this world is to observe, to spy, to watch, to scrutinize oneself and others, to be nothing but a big, slightly vitreous, somewhat bloodshot, unblinking eye."[3]

The Eye was followed by *Glory* (1933/1971),

NOVELS

which recounts the odyssey of Martin Edelweiss, the son of a Swiss father and Russian mother. "Martin," according to Nabokov, "is the kindest, uprightest, and most touching of all my young men."[4] Begun in memory and ending in mystery, *Glory* is the story of Martin's search for identity and purpose. It concludes with his departure for Latvia and a planned secret crossing back into his Russian homeland. Though unevenly written and structurally fragmented, *Glory* contains some of Nabokov's most inspired prose. The original title, *Podvig*, is more properly translated as "exploit." But that word, if mispronounced, gives the wholly inappropriate meaning, "utilize." Nabokov's subject is "the inutile deed of renown" (the novel's working title was "Romantic Times"). The glory in this work refers to "the glory of high adventure and disinterested achievement; the glory of this earth and its patchy paradise; the glory of personal pluck; the glory of a radiant martyr."[5]

Laughter in the Dark (1933/1938), the next novel, is quite different in tone. It is Nabokov's novel of black humor in which the notion "love is blind" is literally embodied. In this most cinematic of Nabokov's novels (brief, fleeting chapters developing a time-worn melodramatic story), Albert Albinus, a middle-aged and married art entrepreneur, is blinded literally as well as figuratively by his passion for Margot, a sixteen-year-old movie-house usherette. The tale ends with his accidental death at Margot's hand. The extensive revisions in the English version of the novel highlight the author's interest in reworking to the fullest the cliché elements of misguided sexual passion and cruel opportunism. In these respects the novel is not unlike *King, Queen, Knave* in tone and narrative interest.

The Real Life of Sebastian Knight (1941), the first of Nabokov's novels written in English, pursues some of the major thematic interests of *The Gift*. It is another exploration into the truth of a life and the nature of art. V, the narrator, seeks to establish the true identity of a half-brother he hardly knew by tracking his past—visiting the places where Sebastian had been, meeting people Sebastian had known, and studying the books Sebastian had written. The reader has independent access to the evidence as well as the narrator's interpretations of it. The knight-like moves of the author (the chess-problem configuration of the text is apparent, beginning with the title) make clear that the reader is expected to come to independent conclusions.

The title of Nabokov's second novel in English, *Bend Sinister* (1947), refers to a heraldic band drawn to the left side. "This choice of title was an attempt to suggest an outline broken by refraction,

NOVELS

a distortion in the mirror of being, a wrong turn taken by life, a sinistral and sinister world."[6] The hero is Adam Krug, philosopher, and the setting is the Ekwilist state ruled over by the dictator, Paduk. As Nabokov has acknowledged, the novel has clear ties with *Invitation to a Beheading*. The central themes are the tortured heart, the brutality of the torturer, and the knowledge (perceived at least by Krug) that all the characters "are merely [the author's] whims and megrims."[7]

Nabokov's last two novels were *Transparent Things* (1972) and *Look at the Harlequins!* (1974). *Transparent Things* is a slim work which explores the idea of reality (life) perceived as a text to be edited. Hugh Person (You, Person), an editor by profession, attempts to revisit his past only to discover that the actuality does not coincide with the memory. Person's attempt to edit the text of his own life is contrasted with texts created by R., the writer whose works Person edits, the text which the narrator is providing, and the grand text of the author.

The narrator of *Look at the Harlequins!* is Vadim Vadimovich N., a well-known Anglo-Russian author whose works include *Pawn Take Queen*, *Slaughter in the Sun*, and *Ardis*. Born in Russia, he is exiled by the Revolution, studies at Cambridge, comes to America, teaches a course on masterpieces of literature. At the age of seventy-one he decides to write his "oblique" autobiography, "oblique because dealing mainly not with pedestrian history but with the mirages of romantic and literary matters."[8] But this is of course not the autobiography of Vladimir Vladimirovich Nabokov. Vadim is a victim of seizures of insanity and is another of Nabokov's unreliable narrators searching for his own identity. At the age of eight his aunt had told him, "'Look at the Harlequins!' "Trees are harlequins, words are harlequins . . . Play! Invent the world! Invent reality!'"[9] Vadim's memoirs, the shadow of his creator's life, offer a tangled world where once again the subjects are reality and identity.

At the time of his death Nabokov had nearly completed another novel, *Original of Laura*. According to the testimony of his son, Dmitri, this work "would have been Father's most brilliant novel, the most concentrated distillation of his creativity, but whose release in incomplete form he expressly forbade."[10]

Stories

Were Nabokov not a novelist he would still deserve great stature as the author of fifty-eight short stories. He had as much respect for the genre of short fiction as he did for the novel. "Many widespread species of Lepidoptera produce small, but not necessarily stunted, races above timberline," he wrote. "In relation to the typical novel the short story represents a small Alpine, or Polar, form. It looks different, but it is conspecific with the novel and is linked to it by intermediate clines."[11] Each of his stories is fully crafted and because of limited length each can be more readily apprehended in its entirety than the novels. Nabokov's own favorites—a good representative selection—were "Spring in Fialta" (1936), "Cloud, Castle, Lake" (1937), "Signs and Symbols" (1948) and "The Vane Sisters" (1959).

Fialta is an amalgam of Yalta, the Crimean resort, and *fialka*, Russian for "violet." The story's title summons to mind the Yalta setting of Chekhov's well-known tale of summer love, "The Lady with the Little Dog." In Nabokov's love story the narrator offers a mosaic composed of past recollections and present events through which he searches for the shape and meaning of his love for Nina, a woman who over fifteen years has moved intermittently in the margins of his life. Relying largely on memory, "that long-drawn sunset shadow of one's personal truth,"[12] he only comes to understand her place in his life and her effect on

his consciousness on the very same day Nina is
driven off to her death.

"Cloud, Castle, Lake," preceding *Invitation to
a Beheading* by two years, gave that novel its title
and shares with it a world of mindless terror. The
story relates the experiences of Vasili Ivanovich,
the narrator's "representative," who has been
obliged to take a "pleasantrip" to the countryside.
To the roar of his companions' voices ("In a paradise of heather,/ Where the field mouse screams
and dies,/ Let us march and sweat together/ With
the steel-and-leather guys!"), Vasili embarks on a
voyage of pain and discovery.[13] Freeing himself at
one point from companions who have merged
together "forming one collective, wobbly, many-
handed being, from which one could not escape,"[14] Vasili experiences a transcendental vision.
Framed in the window of a nondescript room he
glimpses cloud, castle, and lake conjoined in "the
motionless and perfect correlation of happiness"
and offering him "help, promise, and consola-
tion."[15] But Vasili is dragged off while crying out in
despair, "this is nothing less than an invitation to a
beheading."[16] At the story's close the badly beaten
narrator's representative begs for his freedom, and
his narrator, surprisingly, relents and sets him
free.

"Signs and Symbols" is ostensibly a brief

STORIES

tragic story about an elderly couple and their deranged son. The young man suffers from "referential mania," a mental disorder in which "the patient imagines that everything happening around him is a veiled reference to his personality and existence."[17] The detailed description of the malady employs the words "signs," "alphabet," "patterns," "messages," "cipher," "theme," "observers." It is the language not only of medical diagnosis but also of literature and literary criticism. The inference which can be drawn is that "referential mania" can also be an affliction of readers who get caught up in an over-reading of a literary text.

"Signs and Symbols" not only suggests the possibility, but exemplifies, through a perfect merging of form and content, just how that might come about. The reader learns that the son has been in the asylum for four years and that he has tried several times to take his life. It is his birthday and his elderly parents try to visit him, only to be told that he has once again attempted suicide. They leave without seeing him, greatly saddened and wondering if one day they might bring him home. Past midnight, "an unusual hour for their telephone to ring," they receive two calls, both wrong numbers. As the story ends the phone rings a third time. It is left to the reader to decide what is the import of the last call. In effect, the reader must complete the story according to his interpretation of the text. Is it another wrong number? Or are there a sufficient quantity of ominous details in the text to conclude that the call will announce the son's death. Whatever the reader decides, Nabokov is demonstrating one way in which a reader is made the author's accomplice.

"The Vane Sisters," the last story that Nabokov wrote, details the narrator's place in the lives and afterlives of Cynthia and Sybil Vane. Both sisters have died, Sybil by suicide and Cynthia from a heart attack. The narrator, a sceptic concerning Cynthia's interest in spiritualism, seeks "to refute and defeat the possible persistence of discarnate life"[18] by challenging the dead Cynthia to communicate with him. As the story opens the narrator is "in a state of raw awareness that seemed to transform the whole of my being into one big eyeball rolling in the world's socket."[19] He has not yet learned that Cynthia has died as he walks about engaging in an intense investigation of the "trivia" of the morningscape. He is fascinated, in particular, by the trickles of water rhythmically falling from a family of icicles. This "trivial" detail of the morning combines with the last paragraph to give the key to the story. Nabokov was very proud

TRANSLATIONS

of this closing, unnoticed by the narrator, which forms an acrostic whose solution provides a startling conclusion to the tale.

Translations

In one sense, the act of writing is the act of translating the material of imagination into the medium of words. Nabokov did this with rare brilliance in three different languages. But he was also, throughout his career, the translator of other's works. He translated into Russian from French and English (Rolland, Ronsard, Verlaine, Supervielle, Baudelaire, Rimbaud, Musset, Yeats, Carroll, Byron, Tennyson, Shakespeare), into French from Russian (Pushkin), and into English from Russian (*The Song of Igor's Campaign*, Pushkin, Lermontov, Tiutchev, Fet, Khodasevich). Over the years his method evolved more and more towards precise literality of transposition. The evolution is best exemplified in a comparison of his 1923 translation of Lewis Carroll's *Alice in Wonderland* and his 1964 translation of Alexander Pushkin's *Eugene Onegin*.

In the earlier work he Russified Carroll's classic by turning Alice into Anya (she is the un-Russian "Alisia" in all other translations) and then making her comprehensible to a young Russian reader. Rather than translating literally at every point, he adapted characters and narrative, as needed, into Russian forms and moved the setting to Russia. The result was a brilliant rendition which is reputed to be the finest translation of *Alice* into any language. Several decades later, after years of arduous labor on *Eugene Onegin*, his views had evolved into the conviction that the only worthwhile translation was a scrupulously literal one. His rendition of *Onegin* sacrifices rhyme and fluidity to the greater demands of precision. It is a work which immediately irritated and continues to irritate those readers who much prefer adaptations that read smoothly, regardless of their fidelity to the original.

Nabokov's practice of translation is of interest to the student of his fiction for several reasons. Being enormously adept in three tongues, aware of the differing ranges of expression particular to each, he knew well the impossibility of carrying over a work, entirely intact, from one language to another. As a writer who valued the precision of his own words and images, he had equally unwavering respect for the integrity of the words of others. It is easy to see why his methodology evolved as it did. He approached the task of translation in the manner in which he hoped translators would approach his own writings.

The first requisite for competent translation is an intelligent, informed, even inspired comprehension of the work to be translated. One has to understand a writer's use of language before one can hope to render his work in a different tongue. When a writer has a dozen synonyms to work with, the translator has to know why one was picked and not another. Nabokov's translations demonstrate his unique knowledge of the style of those he translated, as well as his ability to find the nearest equivalents in other languages. Equally important, the autotranslations of his own prose provide an important body of matter for the study of his own style, since by his selection of equivalents in a second language he reveals the intention of the original. To follow closely as he moves from one language to another is to be welcomed into the writer's workshop as a privileged visitor.

Lectures

When asked to describe his audience, Nabokov replied, "I write for myself and hope for hundreds of little Nabokovs."[20] Such ideal readers, one supposes, would share Nabokov's literary

OTHER WORKS

tastes and values and have a complete understanding of his art. Nabokov never hesitated to express his likes and dislikes in numerous interviews, but he was reticent when asked to "explain" his art. The best source of information on his literary tastes, values, and indirectly on his own art (aside form his memoirs) is found in his classroom lectures. Nabokov taught at Wellesley College and Cornell University, with guest stints elsewhere, from 1941 through 1958. Following his death, and thanks to the far-sighted decision of the Nabokov estate, his handwritten lectures, lecture notes, and marginally annotated classroom texts were gathered, edited and published in several volumes.

The majority of the lectures were delivered in his Cornell course, "Masters of European Fiction," in which he treated Austen's *Mansfield Park*, Dickens' *Bleak House*, Gogol's *Dead Souls*, Flaubert's *Madame Bovary*, Stevenson's *Dr. Jekyll and Mr. Hyde*, Tolstoy's *Anna Karenina*, Proust's *The Walk by Swann's Place*, Kafka's "The Metamorphosis," and Joyce's *Ulysses*. It is to these lectures that the reader who would like to understand his art should turn. In demonstrating how Nabokov read others, they reveal how one should read Nabokov. The lectures are replete with lengthy quotations from the texts being taught, but not because Nabokov had little of his own to say about the texts. The constant

LECTURES

reference to the author's words affirms the primacy of the text, Nabokov's aversion to paraphrase, his stressing of the writer's specifics, and his abhorrence of sweeping generalities.

Nabokov was concerned with the literariness of literature, its matter and substance. He demanded the close intimacy with texts that could come only from careful rereading. Focusing on the smallest details of language, style, motifs, and structure he led his students page by page through the artfulness of selected masterpieces. His aims as a teacher were explained in his concluding lecture: "I have tried to teach you to read books for the sake of their forms, their visions, their art. I have tried to teach you to feel a shiver of artistic satisfaction, to share not the emotions of the people in the book but the emotions of its author—the joys and difficulties of creation. We did not talk around books, about books; we went to the center of this or that masterpiece, to the live heart of the matter."[21]

His overriding concern with specific details in the works of others was much more than a pedagogue's tic, just as the elaborate figuring of detailed worlds in his own fictions is much more than flashy virtuosity. In his art, as in his life, Nabokov always extolled "the supremacy of the detail over the general, of the part that is more alive than the whole, of the little thing which a man observes and greets with a friendly nod of the spirit while the crowd around him is being driven by some common impulse to some common goal. This capacity to wonder at trifles . . . these asides of the sprit, these footnotes in the volume of life are the highest forms of consciousness, and it is in this childishly speculative state of mind, so different from commonsense and its logic, that we know the world to be good."[22]

Notes

1. Vladimir Nabokov, *King, Queen, Knave* (New York: McGraw-Hill, 1968) vii.

2. Vladimir Nabokov, *The Eye* (New York: Phaedra, 1965) 113.

3. *The Eye* 113.

4. Vladimir Nabokov, *Glory* (New York: McGraw-Hill, 1971) x.

5. *Glory* xiii.

6. Vladimir Nabokov, *Bend Sinister* (New York: Time Life Books, 1964) xii.

7. *Bend Sinister* xiv.

8. Vladimir Nabokov, *Look at the Harlequins!* (New York: McGraw-Hill, 1974) 85.

9. *Look at the Harlequins!* 8-9.

10. Dmitri Nabokov, "On Visiting Father's Room" in Peter Quennell, ed. *Vladimir Nabokov. A Tribute* (New York: Viking Press, 1980) 131.

11. From unpublished personal correspondence with this writer, October 22, 1971.

12. Vladimir Nabokov, *Nabokov's Congeries*, ed. Page Stegner (New York: Viking Press, 1968) 131.

OTHER WORKS

13. *Nabokov's Congeries* 103.

14. *Nabokov's Congeries* 103.

15. *Nabokov's Congeries* 106.

16. *Nabokov's Congeries* 107.

17. *Nabokov's Congeries* 174.

18. *Nabokov's Congeries* 228.

19. *Nabokov's Congeries* 214.

20. John G. Hayman, "A Conversation with Vladimir Nabokov—with Digressions," *Twentieth Century* Dec. 1959: 445.

21. Vladimir Nabokov, *Lectures on Literature*. ed. Fredson Bowers (New York: Harcourt Brace Jovanovich / Bruccoli Clark, 1981) 381–82.

22. *Lectures on Literature* 373–74.

CONCLUSION

Vladimir Nabokov's achievements extend into several areas. As a lepidopterist he contributed a new methodology and system of nomenclature for the identification of species. As a practicing multilingual translator he demonstrated the possibility and necessity of maintaining the highest degree of textual accuracy. As a scholar he extended the knowledge of Russian and European literary classics and provoked a reevaluation of the Russian literary tradition. As a teacher he probed the secrets of literary creation and refined the art of reading.

Among his major achievements was the emphatic demonstration that the genre of the novel remains vibrantly alive, despite the periodic, but premature, announcements of its demise. In an array of lucidly written novels Nabokov identified and then proceeded to revive overworked elements of narration, theme, character, and style.

CONCLUSION

His creative and innovative strategies in the deployment of these components rejuvenated the genre and moved the modern novel into new directions. The adulterer's tale, the romance, the detective story, the family chronicle, the confession have all been revivified through the powers of his art.

Nabokov's novels will discomfort readers who are more at home with edifying stories, large doses of dialogue, sweeping generalities, and the amorphous platitudes of a shared, general reality. Instead of offering up easy, average worlds, Nabokov's fictions present the worlds of possibility which only individual fully conscious life can probe, discover and reveal. Nabokov was an iconoclast and innovator, and though his art is difficult, the rewards are great for readers ready to extend the effort they require. An implacable enemy of banality and the commonplace, Nabokov adhered steadfastly to the values of independence, uniqueness, and originality. In an age which more and more compels conformity of every sort, not the least of Nabokov's accomplishments was his unwavering defense of responsible individuality in artistic expression as well as in life.

BIBLIOGRAPHY

I. Memoirs by Nabokov

Conclusive Evidence. New York: Harper, 1951: retitled as
 Speak, Memory. London: Gollancz, 1951: translated as
 Drugie Berega [Other shores]. New York: Chekhov, 1954;
 revised as *Speak, Memory : An Autobiography Revisited*. New
 York: Putnam's, 1967; London: Weidenfeld and Nicolson,
 1967.

II. Letters of Nabokov

Karlinsky, Simon, ed. *The Nabokov-Wilson Letters. 1940–1971*.
 New York: Viking, 1977; London: Weidenfeld and
 Nicolson, 1979.
Nabokov, Vladimir. *Perepiska s sestroi* [Correspondence with
 My Sister]. Ann Arbor, MI. Ardis, 1984.

III. Novels by Nabokov

All of Nabokov's Russian works (1920–1940) were published
under pseudonyms. The Russian novels appeared under the
name "V. Sirin."

Mashen'ka. Berlin: Slovo, 1926; translated as *Mary* by Michael
 Glenny in collaboration with the author. New York:
 McGraw-Hill, 1970; London: Weidenfeld and Nicolson,
 1971.
Korol', dama, valet. Berlin: Slovo, 1928; translated as *King,
 Queen, Knave* by Dmitri Nabokov in collaboration with the
 author. New York: McGraw-Hill, 1968; London:
 Weidenfeld and Nicolson, 1968.
Zashchita Luzhina. Berlin: Slovo, 1930, translated as *The De-
 fense* by Michael Scammell in collaboration with the au-
 thor. New York: Putnam's, 1964; London: Weidenfeld and
 Nicolson, 1964.

BIBLIOGRAPHY

Soglyadatai. Paris: Russkie Zapiski, 1938; translated as *The Eye* by Dmitri Nabokov in collaboration with the author. New York: Phaedra, 1965; London: Weidenfeld and Nic olson, 1966.

Podvig. Paris: Sovremennye Zapiski, 1932; translated as *Glory* by Dmitri Nabokov in collaboration with the author. New York: McGraw-Hill, 1971; London: Weidenfeld and Nicolson, 1972.

Kamera Obskura. Paris: Sovremennye Zapiski, 1933; trans- lated as *Camera Obscura* by Winifred Roy in collaboration with the author. London: John Long, 1936; translated again as *Laughter in the Dark* by the author. Indianapolis: Bobbs-Merrill, 1938; London: Weidenfeld and Nicolson, 1961.

Otchayanie. Berlin: Petropolis, 1936; translated as *Despair* by the author. London: John Long, 1937; translated again by the author under same title, New York: Putnam's, 1966; London: Weidenfeld and Nicolson, 1966.

Priglashenie na kazn'. Paris: Dom Knigi, 1938; translated as *Invitation to a Beheading* by Dmitri Nabokov in collaboration with the author. New York: Putnam's, 1959; London: Weidenfeld and Nicolson, 1960.

Dar. Paris: Sovremennye Zapiski, Nos. 63-67, 1937–1938 (chapter 4 omitted); first complete edition, New York: Chekhov, 1952; translated as *The Gift* by Michael Scammel in collaboration with the author. New York: Putnam's, 1963; London: Weidenfeld and Nicolson, 1963.

The Real Life of Sebastian Knight. Norfolk, CT: New Directions, 1941; London: Editions Poetry, 1945.

Bend Sinister. New York: Holt, 1947; London: Weidenfeld and Nicolson, 1960.

Lolita. Paris: Olympia Press, 1955; New York: Putnam's, 1958; London: Weidenfeld and Nicolson, 1959.

BIBLIOGRAPHY

Pnin. Garden City, New York: Doubleday, 1957; London: Heinemann, 1957.

Pale Fire. New York: Putnam's, 1962; London: Weidenfeld and Nicolson, 1962.

Ada or Ardor: A Family Chronicle. New York: McGraw-Hill, 1969; London: Weidenfeld and Nicolson, 1969.

Transparent Things. New York: McGraw-Hill, 1972; London: Weidenfeld and Nicholson, 1973.

Look at the Harlequins! New York: McGraw-Hill, 1974; London: Weidenfeld and Nicolson, 1975.

IV. Collected Poems, Stories, and Plays by Nabokov

Stikhi [Poems]. St. Petersburg, Russia: Privately printed in 500 copies, 1916.

Al'manakh. Dva puti [An Almanac. Two Paths] [poems]. With Andrei Balashov. Petrograd, Russia: Privately printed in 500 copies, 1918.

Grozd'. Stikhi [The Cluster. Poems], under the pseudonym, "V. Sirin." Berlin: Gamaiun, 1923.

Gornii put' [The Empyrean Path] [poems], under the pseudonym, "V. Sirin." Berlin: Grani, 1923.

Vozvrashchenie Chorba. rasskazy i stikhi [*The Return of Chorb: Stories and Poems*], under the pseudonym, "V. Sirin." Berlin: Slovo, 1930.

Izobretenie Val'sa. Paris: Russkie zapiski, No. 11, 1938; translated as *The Waltz Invention: A Play in Three Acts* by Dmitri Nabokov. New York: Phaedra, 1966.

Nine Stories, translated by the author or in collaboration with the author. New York: New Directions, 1947.

Stikhotvoreniia 1929–1951 [Poems 1929–1951]. Paris: Rifma, 1952.

BIBLIOGRAPHY

Vesna v Fial'te i drugie rasskazy [Spring in Fialta and Other Stories]. New York: Chekhov, 1956.

Nabokov's Dozen: A Collection of Thirteen Stories, three stories originally written in Russian translated by Peter Pertzov in collaboration with the author. New York: Doubleday, 1958; London: Heinemann, 1959.

Poems. New York: Doubleday, 1959; London, Weidenfeld and Nicolson, 1961.

Nabokov's Quartet [stories], three stories originally written in Russian translated by Dmitri Nabokov. New York: Phaedra, 1966; London, Weidenfeld and Nicolson, 1967.

Poems and Problems, translated by the author. New York: McGraw-Hill, 1971; London: Weidenfeld and Nicolson, 1972.

A Russian Beauty and Other Stories, title story translated by Simon Karlinsky and the others by Dmitri Nabokov, all in collaboration with the author. New York: McGraw-Hill, 1973; London: Weidenfeld and Nicolson, 1973.

Lolita. A Screenplay. New York: McGraw-Hill, 1974.

Tyrants Destroyed and Other Stories, translated by Dmitri Nabokov in collaboration with the author. New York: McGraw-Hill, 1975; London: Weidenfeld and Nicolson, 1975.

Details of a Sunset and Other Stories, translated by Dmitri Nabokov in collaboration with the author. New York: McGraw-Hill, 1976; London: Weidenfeld and Nicolson, 1976.

Stikhi [Poems]. Ann Arbor, MI: Ardis, 1979.

The Man from USSR and Other Plays, translated by Dmitri Nabokov. San Diego and New York: Harcourt Brace Jovanovich / Bruccoli Clark, 1984; London: Weidenfeld and Nicolson, 1984.

The Enchanter, translated by Dmitri Nabokov. New York:

BIBLIOGRAPHY

Putnam's, 1986; London: Picador/Pan, 1986; from the unpublished Russian manuscript entitled, "Volshebnik," written 1939.

V. Nonfiction by Nabokov

Nikolai Gogol. New York: New Directions, 1944; London: Editions Poetry, 1947.

Strong Opinions [interviews, letters-to-the-editor, essays, reviews]. New York: McGraw-Hill, 1973; London: Weidenfeld and Nicolson, 1974.

Lectures on Literature. Fredson Bowers, ed. New York: Harcourt Brace Jovanovich / Bruccoli Clark, 1980; London: Weidenfeld and Nicolson, 1981.

Lectures on Ulysses. Facsimile of the Manuscript. Columbia, South Carolina: Bruccoli Clark, 1980.

Lectures on Russian Literature. Fredson Bowers, ed. New York: Harcourt Brace Jovanovich / Bruccoli Clark, 1981; London: Weidenfeld and Nicolson, 1982.

Lectures on Don Quixote. Fredson Bowers, ed. San Diego and New York: Harcourt Brace Jovanovich / Bruccoli Clark, 1983; London: Weidenfeld and Nicolson, 1983.

VI. Translations by Nabokov

Nikolka Persik. Translation of Romain Rolland, *Kolas Breugnon.* Berlin: Slovo, 1922.

Ania v strane chudes. Translation of Lewis Carroll, *Alice in Wonderland.* Berlin: Gamaiun, 1923.

Three Russian Poets: Selections from Pushkin, Lermontov and Tyutchev. New York: New Directions, 1945; London: Lindsay Drummond, 1947.

A Hero of Our Time. Translation of Mikhail Lermontov's *Geroi nashego vremeni.* New York: Doubleday, 1958; London: Heinemann, 1959.

BIBLIOGRAPHY

The Song of Igor's Campaign. An Epic of the Twelfth Century.
Translated from Old Russian. New York: Random House
Vintage, 1960; London: Weidenfeld and Nicolson, 1961.

Eugene Onegin: A Novel in Verse by Aleksandr Pushkin. Translated from the Russian, with Commentary. Four volumes.
Bollingen Series LXXII. New York: Bollingen Foundation,
1964; London: Routledge & Kegan Paul, 1964; first revised
edition, Bollingen Foundation, 1974; second revised edition, Bollingen Foundation / Princeton University Press,
two volumes paperback, 1981.

*   *   *

Nabokov is one of the most studied contemporary authors.
The full bibliography of critical writings on his works in various languages includes tens of monographs and unpublished dissertations, and hundreds of articles, essays, and
reviews. Cited here are the books and volumes of collected
criticism written entirely or primarily in English. Additional
citations will be found in the bibliographies which are in-
cluded in most books of criticism.

VII. Biographies of Nabokov

Field, Andrew. *Nabokov: His Life in Part.* New York: Viking,
Press, 1977. An idiosyncratic and often unreliable work.
———. *VN: The Life and Art of Vladimir Nabokov.* New York:
Crown, 1986. An even more unreliable biography than the
first version.

VIII. Books about Nabokov

Appel, Alfred, Jr., ed. *The Annotated Lolita.* With Preface,
Introduction, and Notes. New York: McGraw-Hill, 1970.
Presents the full text of the novel with line by line
annotations.

BIBLIOGRAPHY

————. *Nabokov's Dark Cinema*. New York: Oxford University Press, 1974. Focuses on Nabokov's writings in relation to the movies and popular culture.

Bader, Julia. *Crystal Land: Artiface in Nabokov's English Novels*. Berkeley, CA: University of California Press, 1972. Textual analysis of the first six English novels emphasizing the theme of artistic creation.

Boyd, Brian. *Nabokov's ADA: The Place of Consciousness*. Ann Arbor, MI: Ardis, 1984. Exceptionally fine book which provides not only the best commentary on the novel, but also a most perceptive overview of Nabokov's art in general.

Cancogni, Annapaola. *The Mirage in the Mirror: Nabokov's ADA and Its French Pre-Texts*. New York: Garland, 1985. Examination of the allusive networks in Nabokov's fiction; concentrates on *Ada*.

Clancy, Laurie. *The Novels of Vladimir Nabokov*. New York: St. Martin's Press, 1984. Overview of the novels.

Clark, Beverly Lyon. *Reflections of Fantasy. The Mirror Worlds of Carroll, Nabokov, and Pynchon*. New York: Peter Lang, 1986. Explores the technique of the mirror-world in the works of these three authors.

Field, Andrew. *Nabokov: His Life in Art*. Boston: Little, Brown, 1967. An overview of all of Nabokov's writings, fiction and nonfiction, through *Pale Fire*.

Fowler, Douglas. *Reading Nabokov*. Ithaca, NY: Cornell University Press, 1974. Attempts to reduce Nabokov's fictions to four thematic, moral, and narrative constants through the examination of three stories and five novels.

Grayson, Jane. *Nabokov Translated. A Comparison of Nabokov's Russian and English Prose*. Oxford: Oxford University Press, 1977. Study of Nabokov's practice of autotranslation.

Hyde, G. M. *Vladimir Nabokov: America's Russian Novelist*.

BIBLIOGRAPHY

Critical Appraisal Series. London: Marion Boyars, 1977.
Well-balanced overview of all the novels, with particular
reference to their place in the Russian literary tradition.

Johnson, D. Barton. *Worlds in Regression: Some Novels of
Vladimir Nabokov.* Ann Arbor, MI: Ardis, 1984. Important
study of the intricate patterns of Nabokov's fiction; treats
eight novels and the autobiography.

Karges, Joann. *Nabokov's Lepidoptera: Genres and Genera.* Ann
Arbor, MI: Ardis, 1984. Examination of butterflies in
Nabokov's fiction.

Lee, L. L. *Vladimir Nabokov.* Twayne's United States
Author's Series, Nr. 266. Boston: Twayne, 1976. General
overview of Nabokov's novels.

Lokrantz, Jessie T. *The Underside of the Weave: Some Stylistic
Devices Used by Vladimir Nabokov.* Uppsala, Swed.: Acta
Universitatis Upsaliensis. Studia Anglistica Nr. 11, 1973.

Long, Michael. *Marvell, Nabokov: Childhood and Arcadia.* Oxford: Oxford University Press, 1984.

Mason, Bobbie Ann. *Nabokov's Garden: A Guide to ADA.* Ann
Arbor, MI: Ardis, 1974. Critique of the novel as "an inversion of the story of Eden" through examination of its nature imagery.

Milbauer, Asher Z. *Transcending Exile: Conrad, Nabokov, I. B.
Singer.* Miami: Florida International University Press, 1985.
Examination of the theme of exile in *Mary*, *The Real Life of
Sebastian Knight*, and *Pnin*.

Morton, Donald E. *Vladimir Nabokov.* New York: Ungar,
1978. Survey of the English novels.

Moynahan, Julian. *Vladimar Nabokov.* Pamphlets on American Writers, Nr. 96. Minneapolis: University of Minnesota
Press, 1971. Brief treatment of several selected novels.

Nakhimovsky, A. and S. Paperno, eds. *An English-Russian
Dictionary of Nabokov's LOLITA.* Ann Arbor, MI: Ardis,

BIBLIOGRAPHY

1982. Helpful volume for those interested in Nabokov's language usage and stylistics.

Naumann, Marina T. *Blue Evenings in Berlin. Nabokov's Short Stories of the 1920s.* New York: New York University Press, 1978. Presents close readings of nineteen of Nabokov's earliest Russian stories.

Packman, David. *Vladimir Nabokov. The Structure of Literary Desire.* Columbia, MO: University of Missouri Press, 1982. Post-structuralist treatment of *Lolita*, *Ada*, and *Pale Fire*.

Pifer, Ellen. *Nabokov and the Novel.* Cambridge, MA: Harvard University Press, 1980. Study of the moral underpinnings of Nabokov's fictional worlds.

Proffer, Carl. *Keys to LOLITA.* Bloomington, IN: University of Indiana Press, 1968. Annotations to the text; a good companion volume to *The Annotated Lolita*.

Rampton, David. *Vladimir Nabokov: A Critical Study of the Novels.* Cambridge, Eng: Cambridge University Press, 1984. Overview of the novels.

Ross, Stanley. *Vladimir Nabokov: Life, Work and Criticism.* Fredericton, Can: York Press, 1985.

Rowe, William W. *Nabokov's Deceptive World.* New York: New York University Press, 1971. Study of some stylistic devices in Nabokov's fiction; includes the controversial section on sexual symbols to which Nabokov objected.
———. *Nabokov's Spectral Dimension.* Ann Arbor, MI. Ardis, 1981. Attempts to identify spectres and spirits in Nabokov's fiction.

Stegner, Page. *Escape Into Aesthetics: The Art of Vladimir Nabokov.* New York: Dial Press, 1966. Pioneering study of the English novels.

Stuart, Dabney. *Nabokov. The Dimensions of Parody.* Baton Rouge: Louisiana State University Press, 1978. Treatment of parody as the configuring feature of several novels.

BIBLIOGRAPHY

Tammi, Pekka. *Problems of Nabokov's Poetics: A Narratological Analysis*. Helsinki, Fin.: Suomalainen Tiedeakatemia, 1985. Study of the narrative manifestations of thematic dominants in the works.

IX. Collected Criticism about Nabokov

Appel, Alfred Jr., and Charles Newman, eds. *Nabokov: Criticism, Reminiscences, Translations, and Tributes*. Evanston, IL: Northwestern University Press, 1970. Important collection of materials dedicated to Nabokov on the occasion of his seventieth birthday.

Couturier, Maurice, ed. *Delta. Vladimir Nabokov*. Special Issue. Montpellier, France: Université Paul Valéry, No. 17, October 1983. Previously unpublished articles on a variety of topics; five in English and four in French.

Dembo, L. S., ed. *Nabokov: The Man and His Work*. Madison, WI: University of Wisconsin Press, 1967. Outstanding collection of critical essays; includes an important checklist of Nabokov criticism in English.

Gibian, George and Stephen Jan Parker, eds. *The Achievements of Vladimir Nabokov. Essays, Studies, Reminiscences, and Stories*. Ithaca, NY: Center For International Studies, Cornell University, 1984. Collection of the various contributions to the Nabokov Commemorative Festival held at Cornell University.

Johnson, D. Barton, ed. *Nabokov Issue. Canadian-American Slavic Studies*, (Fall 1985). Collection of articles on Nabokov's writings by non-American critics.

Page, Norman, ed. *Nabokov: The Critical Heritage*. London: Routledge & Kegan Paul, 1982. Anthology of book reviews of Nabokov's works published in the English-speaking world, 1934-1977.

BIBLIOGRAPHY

Parker, Stephen Jan, ed. *The Nabokovian.* Lawrence: University of Kansas, 1984–; earlier entitled *The Vladimir Nabokov Research Newsletter*, 1978–1984. A semi-annual journal devoted to Nabokov studies; includes notes, abstracts, inquiries, annotations, bibliographies, interviews, photographic documents.

Proffer, Carl, ed. *A Book of Things About Vladimir Nabokov.* Ann Arbor, MI: Ardis, 1974. Fine eclectic collection of essays, annotations, calendars and other things.

Quennell, Peter, ed. *Vladimir Nabokov: A Tribute. His Life, His Work, His World.* London: Weidenfeld and Nicholson, 1979. Collection of previously unpublished essays, articles, reminiscences, and interviews; includes Dmitri Nabokov's notable tribute to his father.

Rivers, J. E. and Charles Nicol, eds. *Nabokov's Fifth Arc: Nabokov and Others on His Life's Work.* Austin, TX: University of Texas Press, 1982. Excellent collection of previously unpublished essays, articles, and notes.

Ross, Charles S., ed. *Modern Fiction Studies: Special Nabokov Issue.* 25 (Autumn 1979). Collection of seven previously unpublished articles, several notes and reviews, and a helpful checklist of Nabokov criticism.

Roth, Phyllis, ed. *Critical Essays on Vladimir Nabokov.* Boston: G. K. Hall, 1984. Collection of some of the finest previously published and unpublished essays treating the full range of Nabokov's writings.

X. Bibliographies

Bryer, Jackson R. and Thomas J. Bergin, Jr. "Vladimir Nabokov's Critical Reputation in English: A Note and a Checklist." In *Nabokov. The Man and His Work.* L. S. Dembo ed. Madison, WI: University of Wisconsin Press,

BIBLIOGRAPHY

1967. Select bibliography of published criticism through 1966.

Field, Andrew. *Nabokov: A Bibliography.* New York: McGraw-Hill, 1973. Bibliography of Nabokov's works in all languages through 1971; has numerous omissions and inaccuracies.

Juliar, Michael. *Vladimir Nabokov: A Descriptive Bibliography.* New York: Garland, 1986. The standard, primary bibliography of Nabokov's writings; includes all works, fiction and nonfiction, translations into all languages, recordings, adaptations, interviews, miscellanea, and various helpful indexes.

Parker, Stephen Jan and others. "Nabokov Annual Bibliography." *The Vladimir Nabokov Research Newsletter* (1978–1984) and *The Nabokovian* (1984–). Lawrence, KS: University of Kansas. Annual updating of Nabokov works and criticism in all languages.

Schuman, Samuel. *Vladimir Nabokov: A Reference Guide.* Boston: G. K. Hall, 1979. Annotated bibliography of Nabokov criticism in English, 1931–1977.

———. "Criticism of Vladimir Nabokov: A Selected Checklist." *Vladimir Nabokov Issue. Modern Fiction Studies.* No. 3 (Autumn 1979).

INDEX

INDEX

INDEX

INDEX

INDEX